DREAM DESIRE DESTINATION

SAURABHI SHAHI

OM NAMAH SHIVAY

This book is dedicated to every person, who dreams and believes in fulfilling them. People dream big but they do not know how to make those dreams come true? This book is dedicated to every person who has dreams in his eyes and has the passion to fulfill those dreams.

One who dreams big and wants to know, what is the formula to make dreams come true? Or one who thinks that success is only in the fate of rich people or only those with good luck are rich and successful.

If you have a dream, to travel the world at a young age, or to buy a sea facing bungalow or to live happily in life, then this book is dedicated to people like you.

This book of mine is dedicated to everyone who knows that every dream can come true if they have a passion to achieve those dreams. Dreams have no age, they only have wings to fly. This book is dedicated to each and every shining eye that dreams and believes in fulfilling it.

There is a power in this universe which enables people to fulfill their dreams, these people know how to go for it but they do not share it with the world. My aim is not just to fulfill my own dream. My dream is to fulfill everyone's dreams. That's why, it is dedicated to all such people, who want such happiness.

It is dedicated to every person who has dreams but they do not know the way to fulfill them and are unaware.

What is the purpose of your life? The one who wants to know? How to reach that point, where he/she feels proud, can make a mark in the world, earn his name and it is his dream to bring glory to his family.

This book is dedicated to everyone who dreams and dreams of flying high in the sky. Now, don't delay, open your wings and get ready to fly.

Let's start this beautiful journey of your dreams.

A journey of dreams, desires and destination.

Saurabhi Shahi

Contents

Contents

Foreword

"Real success is finding your lifework in the work that you love."

- David McCullough

From a simple, reserved, and disciplined girl to an inspiring Author, Saurabhi's journey has been an incredible one. I have seen her grow and evolve in different phases of her life. From excelling at a corporate job to teaching and then to evolve into being an inspiring author, Saurabhi's journey has been a journey of courage, endurance and always moving forward despite obstacles. Her words in the book speak her mind, her words make us dream, have faith, and follow that dream.

This book inspires its readers to dream, explains in simple yet effective terms how dreams are im portant in someone's life to get ahead. As we all know very well, a dream without a tangible plan of action is worthless, this book provides some very insightful methods on how to place a roadmap for achieving the dreams.

The book also explores deeper into the power of belief and positive thinking. Readers are presented with some captivating examples explaining how a positive belief system scales some very daunting and seemingly impossible tasks.

This book also makes us look into others' perspectives through small examples. How time, situation, and parameters are different for different individuals. Which eventually shapes up their perspective. It teaches us to be non-judgmental towards each other. How dreams come in different shapes, sizes, and characters. And we should not judge any person because their dreams are differ ent from ours.

The core theme of the book revolves around happiness, a whole section is dedicated to explaining different nuances of happiness and how everyone seeks happiness in life but wanders behind false goals which eventually make them unhappy and miserable. Readers will be challenged to ponder about what really makes them happy and contemplate if it is really worth chasing the superficial goals they spend their entire life on.

I extend my best wishes to Saurabhi for the excellent incorporation of her experiences. And wish that millions get inspired by her work.

Good luck, Shine bright.

Pragya Prasun Singh,

Nari Shakti Award Winner

Pragya is an Indian activist who survived an acid attack and had set up Atijeevan foundation .The organisation has supported more than 250 other acid survivors and in 2019 she was awarded by Nari shakti Puraskar by the Government of India for recognition of her work. She is an example of courage and a source of inspiration to all. Despite this Pragya never stopped dreaming, and has made all her dreams come true. She became an epitome of hope and courage for many in this country.

Dreams, each one of us have it. You express it or not, we all have big dreams hidden inside us and the same goes with the desires. Have you ever wondered why some people dream big and desire them to be true, and it comes true, while some others just dream and desire but it remains only a thought in their mind and nothing else.

This book is going to give you an insight into how dreams and desires drive a person to the destination i.e., the goal to achieve in life. I really feel honored to write this foreword for Saurabhi as I know she is going to help you to reach your destination.

I liked the analogy and the metaphors she has used in the stories in this book. It will connect you deeply with the stories leaving a mark of good understanding. Saurabhi has used simple English to make the understanding more effective. This book in a nutshell is a recipe for success with all appropriate ingredients in it.

I hope you will get the much-needed wisdom to reach your destination in a simplified yet impactful version.Don't give up your dreams, work on it and let success make all the noise.

I wish her all the best.

Dr. Shanti Roy,

Padamshri Award winner

Dr. Shanti Roy is an Indian Gynaecologist from Bihar. She was graced with the Padma Shri Award in 2020. She has been serving for past five decades, from a time very few women were in the field. She is also an author to many medical books of her field. She is a great source of hope and courage to the younger generation. In her times she has beaten patriarchal system and had studied medicine to

pursue her dreams against all the odds prevailing in the society.

Acknowledgements

This book is a golden opportunity for me to express my gratitude, to all the people who are involved in my life in one way or the other, today I want to thank all of them.

First of all, I will start by thanking my diety " **Lord Shiva.** " I am thankful to **Lord Shiv Shankar Bhole Nath** due to whom I got this knowledge and power to write a book.

"Guru govind dou khade kake lagu paye,
balihari guru aapne govind diyo bataye."

With this verse, I will express my gratitude to my parents, today I am in this world because of them. Both of them are my first teachers. My father always encouraged me and my mother had never let me stop. When I became a mother and I took a break after entering motherhood, my mother always inspired me to keep doing something or the other. Today it is the result of that never-ending passion that I have been able to develop myself as a writer. I did my studies in the field of law and also practiced for some time, then I switched into the world of teaching as a teacher I could balance my personal and professional life and was able to take care of my daughter "Ahana". Unfortunately, I had an accident and I got injured, due to the injury, I was unable to walk. It took me two years to walk properly again. May be, if it had not happened, I would not have been writing today. I am grateful for all the good and bad things that happened in my life, because today if I look back, I understand that if these incidents had not happened, I would not have developed as a writer. I am grateful to all the people who have helped me and inspired me to keep moving forward with their support. I also thank those people who harassed me and prevented me from moving forward, they never missed opportunity to hurt me and may be because of those reasons, I could evolve to become stronger and better, today. I thank all the pressure due to which I was able to transform. Everyone knows, a diamond is nothing but a piece of carbon, which is under the pressure for years and due to that pressure, it has turned into a diamond.

I would like to thank my book coach "**Sweta Samota**" who made me aware of all the small and big things that happen in the field of writing. I thank her wholeheartedly and express my gratitude.

I would like to thank "**Siddharth Shah**" with all my heart. He is my mentor and because of him I have learnt how to live my life. I was able to explore the right way to see life and I am still learning more day- by -day.

I am deeply grateful to my husband ,"**Asmit**" and my daughter,"**Ahana**", who have given me their co-operation and support, due to which, I was able to write this book.

I express my heartfelt gratitude to all my friends and my entire family, who gave me self-confidence, confidence and inspiration to keep moving forward.

I thank "**Pragya Prasun Singh**" and "**Dr. Shanti Roy**" for believing in me.

I thank all of you from the bottom of my heart, who have bought or read this book, and I hope, with this book, you will fulfill your dreams and along with this, you will inspire and encourage many others to read this book.

Lots of gratitude,
Saurabhi Shahi.

CHAPTER ONE

Introduction

Dreams have no age, all they have are wings to fly. No one can dare to say to anybody that dreams have an age restriction, you are old, so stop dreaming. It is totally irrespective of your age, so age has nothing to do with your dreams. You can set the stage on fire with the talent you possess at any time in your life. The viewer's eye sees the talent and not the age.

It's well said, age is just a number, this is what you should remember and nothing else. If age really had anything to do with your dreams, passions, and achievements then all dreamers, achievers that we see today, should always be young and not old. But this is not true, everyone dreams and succeeds. Today, in this age of technology, many children have helped their Grandparents to give flight to their dreams. One such story is of Chandigarh's Barfi Wali Dadi, Dadi's real name is Harbhajan Kaur. She is a resident of Chandigarh. She is 94 years old and four years ago i.e. at the age of 90, she started her Besan ki Barfi business (Harbhajan Kaur Ki Barfi Online) which has become a brand today.

It is very important for a person to have a dream. Life without a dream is of no use. A life without any dream is similar to the animal's life in which they eat, drink, sleep and reproduce. We are born as humans and we should be thankful to God that we have a different life than that of animals. Dreams differ from person to person. Your dream might not excite me and mine, might not excite you. This is absolutely perfect because I am responsible to live my dreams and not yours. What's important is, your dreams should excite you. It should excite you so much that you are consistent in your efforts to achieve them.

So, do dreams judge people? Nah! Not at all. Instead, this burden lies on the shoulders of our society. No matter how well you do, you will be judged. If you are successful in your career, you will be questioned and judged at your personal front and vice versa.

You should never judge any person just because their dreams are different from yours. Dreams come in different shapes, sizes and characters. One might have a dream to be a good housewife and a mother who juggles all day, to provide her family with good food and a well-kept house with well-behaved children, despite her high professional degrees. On the other hand, one might dream to be a dynamic corporate person, who knows every small and big happening of the corporate world but is completely unaware of what is going on, at her home. She might not even be aware of her child's favourite food or a toy. Her house might not be well kept, instead, it's always in a mess. It's perfectly okay in both cases, she should not be judged by anyone, for choices she has made. The thing that matters the most is, you are living your dream, after accomplishing it, you feel satisfied and happy. For some, dreams are associated with material accomplishments, like big bank balance, fancy cars, etc, and for some, it's just a mental state of mind and not the money matters of life.

Dreams should go on and on. The moment you achieve one, you should fill it with a new one very quickly. It gives you a reason to work again, might be in some other direction and with some new ideas towards a new purpose. Every dream has a different way by which it's being fulfilled. In order to fulfil the dream, a person takes up a different path every time and while doing so, explores a plethora of stuff. Sometimes, one explores a few things accidentally and later on cherishes those experiences throughout life in the form of memory. This is the same discovery that you get after making mistakes again and again. When we walk on the path of making dreams come true, we learn a lot from our experiences and mistakes.

It's not necessary that all your dreams come true in a very small span of time, sometimes it takes less time and sometimes decades to come true. Don't get disheartened and drop the mission, if your dreams are taking time to become reality, instead of halting, keep going on, with faith in your heart.There is a runner and a chaser game going on, in between the dreamer and the dreams. Many times, you are close to getting hold of your dreams but it slips off from your hand. You get disappointments but you soon find new ways to get hold of it. Keep this game going on throughout your life.

Thomas Alwa Edison had said while inventing bulb, he had failed 1000 times, so he knows 1000 ways that won't work.

"I have not failed I have just found 1000 ways that won't work."-Thomas Alwa Edison

The time you take to fulfil your dreams depends on the hard work you put in and the strategies you adopt. Sometimes, it's left on life circumstances named "**FATE**", and this becomes "**The biggest hurdle**", of your life. It's not wise to say circumstances are hurdles. Circumstances pop up, just to test your hard work and focus. It's very important that the size of your dream is bigger than the hurdles that come in your way as circumstances. Your dream should be big enough to engulf those hurdles and make a way out of them.

William James has said, "We can change our circumstances by a mere change of our attitude." so, stop blaming circumstances for all the failures in your life.

No wonder the way to success goes through many channels of hardships, if your heart desires to fulfil it, it finds a way. There is a famous proverb,"**where there is a will there is a way.**"Keep the sparkle of your dreams alive and don't let it die. If not now, then later it will come to life. Remember to light the fire within you, if you want to fulfil your desire. Keep dreaming and keep achieving your dreams.

"The future belongs to those who believe in the beauty of their dreams."- Eleanor Roosevelt

CHAPTER TWO

Dream

What is a dream?

A dream is a wonderful human experience, in which the person feels the state of consciousness characterized by sensory, cognitive, and emotional episodes, while in the state of sleep. The dreamer sometimes has control over his dreams and sometimes does not. Dreams are in most cases full of vivid experiences that correspond to our life. Dreams mostly happen when we sleep, and it does not mean it happens only in the state of sleep. Sometimes, the images and pictures come to our mind and we visualize it, as a series of pictures or images in the mind related to that thought even when we are awake, and we slip into visualizing those events and the reel of it plays in our mind just like a movie. This state when we are not asleep and dreaming is often referred to as, "day-dreaming." That's why, I stated that sometimes, we have control over it i.e. while daydreaming and when we are asleep it's beyond our control.

Now the question arises, what is the content of the dream?

The content of our dream is directly proportional to the thoughts of our minds just before we sleep. When we watch a horror movie just before sleeping, we get spooky dreams, when we are stressed or disturbed, we have disturbed emotions and as a result, we get distressing reel playing in our mind in the state of sleep and we feel that disturbing emotions that can be fear, anxiety, trauma and we often tag it as a nightmare or a bad dream. If we broadly classify dreams, they are of two types positive and negative and they are highly affected by the stimulus. The positive triggers result in positive dreams and the negative triggers result in negative dreams.

Let's understand it with this story.

Tara and Sitara were twin sisters and orphans, they were compelled to live with their Grandparents. One stayed with the maternal Grandmother and the other with the paternal Grandmother.

Tara's Grandmother was a retired high school teacher, she was highly intelligent and had knowledge-based stories in her mind. Every night while putting Tara to sleep, she would narrate an inspiring story of a space scientist or of a famous personality, who was very successful in his life. This was a ritual both relished the most, before slipping into the state of sleep. Every day, Tara would listen to the story narrated by her Grandma and would gently slip into the state of sleep. After getting up in the morning, Tara would run to her Grandma, hug her, and say, "Do you know what I dreamt, last night?" Her Grandma would keenly lend her ears to listen to her dream stories. In Tara's stories, most of the time, she would be a scientist or an astronaut. This was not at all surprising to her Grandma, as she could relate, whatever she had narrated last night as a bedtime story had appeared in her granddaughter's dreams.

On the other hand, Sitara's Grandmother was a very religious lady and had a sound knowledge of Indian Mythology. She would cuddle Sitara while in bed and would tell her the bedtime stories of Lord Ram from the Ramayana. Every morning after waking up, Sitara would narrate her dream to her Grandma in which mostly Lord Ram would visit her or Sitara would visit Ayodhya, in her dreams. These two stories are enough to understand the trigger for the dreams. Dreams are mostly connected to the triggers that we get from day-to-day life. If we get positive triggers, we have positive dreams and when it is negative, it is a nightmare.

We often come across people saying, "I have a dream of buying a big fancy car or to be a successful entrepreneur, etc." Here we are talking about the trigger again. Here consciously, a person gives a stimulus to the mind about the fancy-looking car or to a certain position where that person sees himself. It's not part of current life reality right now, but the person aims to be at that point and sees himself in dreams with that particular substance, car, house, or at that position. Here, the dream is closely associated with a particular desire to achieve something. The desire to achieve that particular thing drives that person and puts in the fuel (efforts) to reach his destination. (Goal)

The dream to become reality, is driven by a strong desire in that person, and with the strong desire to make that very dream turn into reality, the person works hard, day and night, 24/7 till the time that dream is achieved, and when the dream is achieved, the person reaches the destination. The moment a dream gets fully filled, it puts the person in a state of ecstasy. For some time, it gives joy to the person, and again as time passes, it becomes a common part of his life and it does not excite him. The gap between dream and reality is filled the moment the dream comes true. Again, the person starts dreaming of something that he does not have and puts that picture in his mind of something that he desires again and this cycle continues and keeps ongoing throughout the life.

The cycle of dream, desire and destination continues throughout life.

To keep this cycle of dream desire and destination going on needs great discipline. I will mention it under different chapters, these chapters are appropriate enough to help any person in making this journey swift. In this cycle of dream, desire, and destination, the most important part is you. Yes, you heard it right, it's you. So, gear up, tighten your seatbelts, I am setting you on a voyage to your better self in the future.

"All your dreams can come true. If you have the courage to pursue them"- Walt Disney

CHAPTER THREE

Make yourself priority

"When the Centre of the circle is defined, the circumference is smooth and round. A circle can be drawn only with a defined centre."Make yourself the centre of the circle.

We have been studying about the solar system since our childhood, and all of us know very clearly that the solar system is a family of the sun and its eight planets, in which the sun is at the centre and has eight planets, asteroids, and meteoroids revolving around it. The sun is at the centre and the family revolves around it.

We have to exactly adapt this irrespective of our gender. Make yourself the centre, if you are taking care of yourself everything will automatically fall into its respective places. In this busy world, when it comes to taking care of yourself the most common problem that pops up is time. Wait for a second, hold on your breath, and ask again.

Is time really the problem?

If it was so, no one would have succeeded in life and this world would have filled itself with morons and idiots but sadly this is not the case. The world is full of wonderful people, who are geniuses in their field. Why are they not falling prey to the crunch of time? Or, are they buying time and that makes their day of 30 hrs instead of 24 hrs. How can anyone buy time? It's impossible. Isn't it?

I might sound very disappointing to you but actually, time is not the problem, as the almighty has given the same number of hours to a common man and even to the top geniuses like Einstein, Steve Jobs, Bill Gates, etc

What differs is, the time management skills?

Yes, you heard it right, it's all about the management of your time.

So, the first step in achieving all your dreams and desires demands to make yourself the priority of your life. In order to do so, you need sixty minutes for yourself daily. It demands an exclusive time slot for yourself. It is only possible, with the habit of prioritizing the work to be done, throughout the day. It should be your number one habit in this journey. Prepare a to-do- list according to the urgency of work to be done. Divide your day into different slots with a dedicated slot for yourself. Try to make sixty minutes of time for yourself. This habit will make you happy and less anxious throughout the day.

It's not the task that causes the worry instead it's the baggage to do so much work throughout the day, cause it. This is what causes all the chaos in the mind and results in anxiety. The moment you note down the task, in the to-do -list, the jumping monkey mind comes to rest, just writing down the chores with a dedicated time slot, sends a signal to the mind that the particular task needs to be done in that slot only, hence it simplifies and puts all running unnecessary thoughts to rest.

(Why monkey mind? monkey mind because a human mind is known as "markata" in yoga, meaning a monkey because of its wandering nature.) This is one way of finding time for yourself by organizing and prioritizing your work with a slot for an appointment for yourself by yourself. "**An appointment for myself and by myself**", should be the motto, to book a slot in your to-do list every day. Some people might say we make a to-do list and still don't find time as they are really workaholics and think giving time to themself will disrupt their productivity. For such people, I would like to take them to their childhood days, when they used to be in school.

The school had a limited number of hours for its operation which was generally 8 AM to 2 PM. These 6 hours (360 minutes) were divided into eight periods of forty minutes each, in which 320 minutes were consumed for classes, remaining 40 minutes were split to be utilized for morning assembly, short break, and long break as 10 minutes, 10 minutes, 20 minutes respectively. In those limited 6 hours whenever any event used to come up, how did you manage your time in those days?

If you have recollected it, then it's good. Yes, in such a scenario the concept of "zero period" used to come into play. The zero period was made by extracting as little as 5 minutes from each period. As the total number of periods were 8 and the time was reduced by 5 minutes, so each period was for 35 minutes instead of 40 minutes and the zero-period created from all these 8 periods was for 40 minutes (5*8=40). This simple maths was used and it worked like magic. Isn't it true? Bring it back to your life. Squeeze out as little as 5 to 10 minutes from all your to-do list slots to make a zero period for yourself.

Out of 24 hrs, 8 hrs we sleep and have 16 hrs in our hands. Out of these 16 hrs, 4 hrs are devoted to daily chores after deducting it, we are left with 12 hrs and if we take 10 minutes from each hour it makes 120 minutes for ourselves. I was talking about 60 minutes but taking out 2 hrs also seems so simple with this technique. Bring this simple math back to your life and see the magic. Use this zero- period, as a golden time of your day and use it for your self-development.

This self-development can be pursuing a hobby, doing exercise to keep yourself fit, walking, yoga or can be as simple as reading a book. It should be something that makes you a better person and you can see the progress when you turn and look back.

Your today should always be better than your yesterday.

Just remember, if there are two ships in the ocean, one sinking and one sailing, which one will you choose? Of course, you will choose the ship that is sailing because it's safe.

The question that arises is, why did you choose that ship?

1. You choose the ship that is sailing because *you want to be safe and you don't want to lose your life.*

2. *You want to be safe not just to save your life but also to help those who are sinking in the other ship.*

One can help others only if you help yourself first by staying safe. Similarly, if you make yourself the priority then only you can help others and contribute to their well-being.

I will also share a miraculous way to increase your productivity in the next chapter so that you work really smart and finish all the tasks before the expected time. This zero- period, will be the hero of your life and will change your life drastically.

Stop making excuses, it is of no use. Passing statements and saying, "I don't have time for myself" is nothing but a great way to procrastinate. Stop the habit of procrastination and bring the zero period back to life and be the hero of your life. Make a shift from a procrastinator to an action-taker and make your life wonderful by helping yourself first.

Remember, you are the biggest and the most important project of your life.

CHAPTER FOUR

Power of sprints.

What is a sprint?

The literal meaning of sprint is to run as fast as you can, over a short distance either in a race or because you are in a hurry, to get to a particular point. A close look highlights two things,

1. Run as fast as you can, show your best efficiency
2. The short distance means a small duration of time.

In other words, the sprint is your best output for that particular task, with your 100% focus on that task, for a limited duration. This type of focus is also referred to as laser light focus.

Let's understand it with this story.

Rudra was a small boy, who used to take tuitions for Maths. He had his tuition classes from 7-8 daily in the evening. He used to go to his tutor's house, to take his classes, by riding his bicycle. Since his Maths tutor stayed in a posh area, Rudra used to lock his cycle after parking it near his tutor's house gate. By the time his classes got over, it used to be dark. One day, a surprise test was taken by his tutor in which Rudra scored100% marks. Scoring full marks was not only the source of joy to him, but it also brought delight to his tutor, and the tutor decided to reward Rudra as a gesture of appreciation so that he stayed motivated in his studies. He gifted Rudra, a pen that was gifted to him by his teacher when he was his age. Rudra was very happy and he kept it in his pocket and joyfully returned home.

After reaching home, he shared this news with his parents and when he fetched the pen in his pocket, it was missing. He rushed outside his gate, to find the pen near his cycle. He was sure that the pen must have slipped out of his pocket while getting down from the cycle. He tried to find the pen near the area, where he had parked the cycle. Finding the pen seemed difficult, under the light of the lamp post. It was already more than ten minutes of struggle in this process of fetching the pen. It was night and as dinner time approached, Rudra's Grandpa walked up to him with an intent to help him.

Seeing him struggling to find the pen that was so important to him, Grandpa realized that it was the insufficient light that was making the task difficult for him. Grandpa gently switched on his flashlight which he always carried with him. Under the focus of the flashlight, Rudra successfully found his lost pen. He hugged his Grandpa with joy. Later, Rudra showed his reward to his parents and had dinner with the family. This little story tells us about the importance of focus. The lost pen was difficult to find in the dim light of the lamp-post but it was easily found when the flashlight was focused in that particular area while searching it.

One more example of focus that I would like to highlight, is the science experiment of the magnifying glass and the sun rays. I am sure, you must have conducted it while studying in school.

Sun Rays are something that we get daily and it's vital for every living thing on this earth but those rays don't burn anything. But the same sun rays, when concentrated at a point with the help of the magnifying glass at a point, puts fire on paper and it gets burnt. Why does this happen? It happens because the energy gets concentrated at a point for a particular time. This is the power of focus; focus increases the efficiency of a person.

So, while doing all the daily chores, keep your focus 100 % on that particular task and see your increased output. It will really blow your mind. We all have an immense amount of energy within but it goes to waste as it is scattered, bring in all energy to a particular point with focus, and see the game-changing in your life.

Multitasking has become a part of everyone's life but it causes harm as while doing so the focus gets divided. Avoid multitasking and try to focus on the individual tasks that are important and see the astounding results. This sprint method will definitely prove to be a powerful fuel in your vehicle and will help you to drive extra miles with the same amount of fuel. This sprint method is very useful as it helps to finish all the tasks before the expected time, making more room for leisure time or the zero period. This sprint method is also called the Pomodoro method.

Focus is really important if you want to understand more about focus, take out your camera and try to click pictures without focusing on a specific object and check the pictures, I am sure you will be disappointed by the result.

"Your life is controlled by what you focus on."-Tony Robbins

CHAPTER FIVE

Power of belief

What is a belief?

Belief is something you accept as true, right, and something that really exists. Basically, it's a mental attitude of acceptance. Hence, belief is totally dependent on what you feed your mind.

The importance of belief can be measured by people, who believe in God and those who don't. Those who believe in God have a strong faith that God will help them sail through the difficult situations of their life and it happens to them, when the tough days get over such people say, God has sailed us smoothly through our rough times. On the other hand, there are people who don't have faith in God and think whatever happens is happening, as it has to happen and nothing can change it. The same is the case with the people, who believe in ghosts and those who don't. Those who believe in it get scared and those who don't, are not at all bothered by its existence.

So, belief is basically built upon the thoughts we feed our mind. These thoughts are the systemic amalgamation of the words that you say to yourself. The words have immense power in it. Words have the power to make and break anyone. The type of words you use, for yourself, has a serious repercussion on you, as an individual. The feeling of security and insecurity is built upon, how you think and the words you use for yourself.

Thoughts are either positive or negative, these thoughts are transformed into words, and each word either good or bad has an energy associated with it, as everything is in the form of energy around us. The question that haunts everyone's mind is, what makes a person positive or negative? It is not at all possible to be 100 percent positive always, we all are human beings and we are driven by various sets of emotions. The positive or negative depends on how many positive thoughts you have and how many negative. The one that has maximum percentage becomes dominant and the one with low numbers is dormant and rises only when it is triggered.

To understand this, let's say there is a glass of water pure and clear, in a glass tumbler that represents positive thoughts. Now, start adding soil to it, pinch by pinch. The moment you add a pinch of soil to it, it becomes unfit for drinking but is still clear. We keep on adding it, even after adding a small amount of soil it looks clear. The moment you increase the amount and add a spoon full of soil to it, the water starts looking muddy and dirty. Here, the soil represents negative thoughts. A glass of water that was pure and clear, some time before is muddy and unclear now. Let's start to add clean water spoon by spoon to it and keep on adding it. When you add a few spoons of pure water in the beginning nothing happens, but as you continue doing it, after some time the glass will be full of clean and pure water.

Here, the empty glass represents the human mind and the soil represents the bad or negative thoughts and water represents good thoughts. You become what you keep adding to it, the stuff that has major contribution reflects in your behaviour, if you feed in positive thoughts again and again and continue doing so, you will be a positive and confident person with positive beliefs and if you add the negative thoughts then you will become a negative and insecure person with the negative beliefs.

One must have a strong and positive self-belief, the moment you start believing in yourself the magic starts happening around you. Everything around us is in the form of energy and is in the form of matter i.e., it's either solid, liquid, or gas hence, it occupies space and has a weight. Whenever you remove anything from any place that space is taken by another substance as it's not possible to create a vacuum. In your mind too, you can't create a vacuum. There has to be something in it, either positive or negative, either constructive or destructive.

There are only these two possibilities: -

1. Take out something
2. Put in something

In the 1st case, when you take out something it creates room for other things, so the moment negative thoughts are shredded it has to be filled again, here you have to be a bit cautious, in putting efforts to fill the space with positive thoughts.

In the 2nd case, when you put in something. Remember, the water and soil experiment narrated above. No matter how negative you are, if you are consistently putting in positive thoughts, there will be a time when the positive will dominate and it will reflect in your personality.

The belief reminds me of the famous story penned down by Rudyard Kipling "The jungle book." It was the story of a fictional character Mowgli, who was raised by the wolves. He was adopted by the wolf parents and was trained as other wolf children were trained. Here, despite being a human, Mowgli considered himself to be part of the pack of wolves. His -beliefs had made him more wolf than a human being. He was wild, as he was raised in the jungle wilderness, he honed the skill of hunting and killing. He was able to communicate in animal language, he ate raw meat and jungle products. Despite being a human, his belief made him a wolf by traits.

It was a fictional read that we all enjoyed but a similar case was spotted in 1872 when a group of hunters were walking through the forest of Uttar Pradesh, they found a pack of wolves running with a human running on all his four limbs. Later, the wolves were hunted and the boy was captured and brought to an orphanage. Attempts were made to make him adapt to the norms of society, but the attempt failed, the belief of being a wolf was instilled and this human named **Sanichar**, was still wild, ate raw uncooked meat, walked on four limbs, sharpened his teeth by gnawing them over bones. He believed to be a wolf and lead a life of a wolf. This story proves that belief is what makes you whatever you want.

In building this belief system for yourself the affirmations play a big role. These affirmations set a solid foundation for you to believe in yourself and prepare you to achieve everything you want. The foundation of your journey for a dream, desire, and destination starts from building a strong self-belief for yourself. When you think, what you want to achieve is real and take action towards it every day with full devotion and feelings, it transforms into reality. It's not magic, it is a result of beliefs and applied actions towards your goals.

It is said in the 3rd law of motion by Newton, "Every action has an equal and opposite reaction."

So, when inputs are put in the form of action it will definitely yield you the results in the same magnitude of inputs given. It's the law and no one in the world can negate this law.

"You are what you believe yourself to be." -Paulo Coelho

CHAPTER SIX

Goal

Life without a goal is a life without a purpose.

The goal, a very common thing in a football match. Why is it called a goal? It is because it is the point where one has to focus. When we focus on that particular area and hit the ball it enters that area marking a goal for that team. In a game when the concentration and devotion are present, the players hit the ball into the goal post and mark the goal. The goal is an integral part of our day-to-day life; it can be small or big. Every person in life should have some goals. A life without a goal is like walking without knowing where to go?

The goal is the foundation of life. Have you ever travelled to any place, without having an aim in mind, where to go? For travelling, a goal is set to reach a particular place from a given place. You start the journey towards a direction with the set idea to reach a given point, and when you reach, you hit your goal. To reach such a point, you also have to decide how to go? So, you prepare a map in your mind. A strategy is made ready for travelling. If you travel by bus or train, you buy tickets for that destination. If you go by your vehicle or on your foot, you go as per the map's direction. The way to reach the destination may differ but you have to set an idea in mind to travel in a particular direction, and to a specific point. In your life too, the goal of life is important, like the destination you want to reach, when you are traveling.

A goal gives you the aim, and with the help of the aim, you thrive to reach the given point. The aim in life provides you with the purpose, without aim, you are like a traveller who travels by sauntering without knowing where to go. In such a case that person reaches a particular point without a purpose. Reaching a point without a motive is a total waste, as one doesn't know what to do after reaching that point. When one travels with a purpose to a particular point, there is a step-by-step strategy planned and a motive attached to it. Reaching that point results in the completion of the motive.

Let's say, you have to go to the market from home. In such a case, there is a goal in mind from home to market. To reach the market you have to walk in a particular direction. If you don't walk in the direction towards the market and take steps towards the garden, you will end up reaching the garden. The importance of aim becomes clear by the example of the game of darts. In the dart game, to hit a particular point, you have to concentrate on a given point on the dartboard. You aim at a point, then throw the dart to hit that particular point. Without aiming at that particular point, if you throw the dart it fails to hit the target. Be it games, travel, or any task, a goal must be set to achieve it. Keeping goals in your mind is really important. So, develop a habit to set your goals.

Life is precious, to make the most of it, every individual must have a set of goals. It gives your life a purpose. Living a life without a purpose is an absolute waste.

Tie your life to some goals and make it fruitful for yourself and others. Add value to your life by adding some goals. Gear up! Pull-on your socks and give your life a new dimension with your goal list. Soon, you will discover a new you.

List atleast 5 goals for yourself every year. Make a goal card and write your goals in it.

"Setting goals is the first step in turning the invisible into visible.-Tony Robbins

CHAPTER SEVEN

Procrastination

Now as you have set your goals and you are ready to take steps to achieve them, with full belief and faith in yourself, you plan to start a new journey from today and suddenly you remember about a party tonight, you set aside the most important task and decide to attend the party, have fun and postpone to work on your dreams from the next day. When the new day begins you put off the alarm and want to rest as you were at a party last night, you got tired as you enjoyed full night, you again postpone working on your goals and shift it to be done from the next day, this cycle continues.

Procrastination is the snooze button that you hit many times in a day, many important tasks are postponed many times without realizing the harm it is doing to you. Broadly speaking two harms are there.

1. Postponement of work that is important thus keeping the baggage of work intact inside your head.
2. Wastage of time in useless and unproductive work.

Procrastination and laziness are twin brothers and like each other's company. They go hand in hand most of the time killing the productivity of the individual.

The obvious reasons why a person procrastinates are either fear of failure to complete the task due to lack of motivation or trying to be a perfectionist. The fear of committing a mistake in a task makes you so anxious that you fear doing and completing the task with a flaw. The pressure of delivering a flawless piece of work results in procrastination. It is also attached to the fear of being judged by other people if the task delivered is not perfect.

The best example of procrastination can be seen when the parents nag their child to perform simple tasks like finishing homework or cleaning their room, you witness a tug of war between children and their parents for having these smallest tasks done by them. The child puts the snooze button to it and keeps on postponing that task till the last moment of the deadline arrives. So much time is wasted in this, by both. In this example, the frog croaks (anxiety of doing work) in two heads and disturbs the peace. To beat this habit, one must eat that frog early in the morning and do the most important task early in the morning else it will croak the whole day. With each passing day, the baggage of doing work will keep delaying your goals. If you want your dreams to be your reality then ditch procrastination.

Don't procrastinate just to fulfil the short-term excitement that fills your dopamine void.

For instance, just being fascinated by a single click of the smartphone pools you into its dopamine kick and keeps you engaged for long hours without letting you realize how much time you have wasted in scrolling the screen and hopping from one application to the other.

Procrastination can be beaten with a discipline to follow the to-do- list.

Prioritizing the work to be done every day, trains the brain to do all important tasks throughout the day according to the set priority and time, it causes less mental chaos, resulting in less anxiety, making you more organized and a productive person.

Associate your tasks with a reward and keep an eye on the reward.

Keep a reward for completing the task on time. It may be small but it is important because the mind gets tricked by the reward. Every time you give yourself a reward the mind gets a signal of victory and these small wins help you to set a daily routine with ease.

Ask for help to complete the work, as it reduces fear of perfection.

Ask for help, when needed to complete the work. It will minimize the frequency of procrastination. Remind yourself procrastination is a block in your dreams and overcoming it will change your life.

In my opinion, procrastination is just like the speed breakers that slows your speed in this journey of your dream to destination. Get over these speed breakers and accelerate yourself towards your goals by ditching procrastination.

Paralyze resistance with persistence and kill procrastination with your actions.

"Procrastination is the grave in which opportunity is buried."

- unknown

CHAPTER EIGHT

Affirmations

Everything on this earth is made up of atoms. Atoms combine to form molecules and molecules combine to form a matter. Everything around us is a matter, their form might vary. Some are solid, some are liquid and others might be in the gaseous state. Every matter has energy and the law of conservation of energy states, ***"energy can neither be created nor be destroyed but it changes its form from one form to another."*** The words we speak in day-to-day life are also a form of energy. Don't underestimate the power of words; they can make you or break you. The words that you say to yourself daily, reinforces that thought in your mind very firmly. Daily positive affirmation gives you daily motivation. It is important to say your affirmations daily to keep your mindset positive.

The daily act of repeating the affirmation is as important as bathing. You take bath daily and it is a part of your daily routine. You have to take bath daily to keep yourself clean, bathing once in ten days makes you dirty, unfit, and stinky. Similarly, if you do affirmations daily, you will keep a positive mindset, otherwise, your thoughts will be negative and your mindset too will be negative.

Good attracts good and bad attracts bad, let's understand this with the example of a dirty dustbin with garbage. The filth and the garbage will attract only dirty stuff like flies and insects. On the other hand, if it is clean and not dirty it will not attract flies and insects. Your thoughts too function in the same manner. If your mind has negative thoughts, it will attract more negativity, there will be a chain of negative thoughts and if it is positive, it will have a chain of positive thoughts. That is why it's important to say your affirmations daily to keep your positive mindset intact.

In this era of technology, there is a bombardment of information and you all suffer anxiety because of this. There is mental baggage of thoughts in your mind. you eat, drink, sleep and get up with gadgets, mainly smartphones. The moment you wake up in the morning, before opening your eyes you try to grab your phone and you check it but this habit is very dangerous.

The moment you get up, you see your phone screen and the negative information in the messages and in the news. The mind gets triggered at that point the moment you see negative news and information, the chain reaction of the thoughts begins and keeps on multiplying throughout the day.

So, just to prevent yourself from any negative triggers in the early hours, develop the habit of saying positive affirmations. Saying positive affirmations every day, as the first thing in the morning will tune in your mind to the positivity.

Few examples of positive affirmations to be practiced daily

1. I am strong.
2. I have a good immune system.
3. I am mentally and physically fit.
4. I am healthy and wealthy.
5. I am safe.

6. I am protected by the divine.
7. I am spreading love and hope in the world.
8. I am courageous and ready to fight the situation.
9. I am grateful to God for protecting me.
10. I am healing myself and the world from all the negativity.

The above-mentioned affirmations are just a few examples, you can frame any sentence for yourself and affirm it.

Take this small dose of saying the Positive Affirmations daily as the first thing in the morning, and see how you change the energy within yourself and around yourself.

Read these stories to make your belief stronger in affirmations.

There was a little boy named Rohan, he was always fascinated by aircraft. Every time he heard the noise that the flying aircraft made, he would run out of his house and gaze at the sky till he spotted the airplane flying and would continue gazing at it until it was out of his sight. Every time this happened, he would say to himself, “one day, I will also fly a fighter plane.”

Right from the tender age of five, till he was seventeen, he did this without fail. Even the family members used to find it silly. After finishing his 12th, he filled the form for joining the defence services with a firm idea to join the Air Force.

Time passed and he prepared well for his exams. Every day he would study and would start the day by writing, “I am in the Air Force”, on the top of the notebook page followed by the practice exercises of the entrance book. He had prepared well for the exams and in a week, the entrance was to be held. Before the entrance exams, his school principal wanted to guide him as he was a retired colonel, he gave him the last minutes tips and Rohan gracefully accepted all his advice but before leaving he turned and said to the principal, " sir, even if there is a single selection from this city, it would be mine and no one else", he just uttered these words firmly and came back home. He also started preparing for the mock interviews and recorded it in his tape recorder as in those days, only cam- coders were available for recording videos, and that used to be very expensive, so he used a tape- recorder. He used to listen to the way he spoke and tried to improve, after listening to it.

Days passed and he gave his exams and a few days later the result was out and it was word to word true to the words he gave to his principal, he was the only one from his city to crack this entrance and was selected for the Air force.

With the sparkle in his eyes, he went to the principal to share this news. The principal was proud to know this. This short story of Rohan is enough to prove the magic of affirmations. Affirmations are nothing but a positive condition that you set for your mind by saying the same things again and again and the mind is trained to think about it even in the subconscious state and strives to achieve it as the mind loves challenges.

Here is another story of Siya, whose belief was built through her affirmations. It was done unknowingly while playing and it built the belief and it came to reality.

There was a little girl, Siya, who lived in Pune. Recently her father got transferred to Delhi, her father joined his new company in the capital city in December. The family continued to live in Pune as the academic session for Siya was not yet over. They were planning to shift to Delhi in April when the new academic session in the schools begins.

The school search was going on for Siya, as the admissions in Delhi were open. simultaneously her finals were, knocking at the door. Siya's mother Sonal, was full of anxiety as the admissions were tough in Delhi Schools and no less than a nightmare. She shortlisted all the reputed schools and filled the form for the top five schools in Delhi.

The main cause of Sonal's worry was the entrance test to be held for the new admission. She started preparing her daughter for her finals as well as the entrance but one subject was the cause of constant worry and that was Hindi. In Maharashtra Hindi starts from grade 1 whereas in Delhi it starts from the nursery, as a result, there was a big gap in the syllabus in both the states.

Keeping her worries aside, she prepared her daughter as much as she could, and finally, in mid-March, both mother-daughter duo flew down to Delhi for the test.

Siya gave the test very comfortably. There were only four seats in that school for grade 3 and around 70 students appeared for the test; this added to Sonal's worry. After reaching Delhi, Siya was having fun with her father. She gave the test comfortably and a day after the test, she flew back to Pune with her mother.

Her finals were conducted as soon as she returned from Delhi. After the exams, the term break had started in Pune, so there were fun days for Siya ahead. Sonal was also busy meeting all her friends one by one before leaving the city. Her mind was stuck in the admission predicament. Just to vent this worry out, she often asked Siya to brush up on the course as the results were not out in Delhi and she might have to sit for the entrance for other schools too. Siya on the other hand had a constant reply, "Don't worry, I will qualify". The same reply came whenever this question was asked.

Siya also started preparing for the new school by buying a new bag, bottle, and pencil box for the school. Sonal, sometimes found this very strange but Siya started living in the feeling of getting admission to that school. She was also spotted writing that school's name in her new notebooks. She was behaving as if it had already happened. This has become her daily ritual from morning till night. She even told her close friends she got admission and mentioned that school's name. She lived in that feeling believing it's true. All these activities done in innocence were also recorded by her mother sometimes and Siya watched the replay of those recordings, in which she fondly mentions the schools' names in which she gave her entrance and wrote in her diary that I study in so and so school in Delhi. Just after two weeks, there was a call from that very reputed school, mentioning, Siya had made through the entrance and the school is waiting for the admission formalities to be completed.

What worked here was just the belief system. The affirmations were made by her, unknowingly while playing, and were repeated every day, fondly with a good feeling and it worked like magic.

Siya was not an extraordinary student nor was she a very hardworking student she was just an average child, but somehow her innocent mind believed something to be true and it came out as a fact. It was not magic. It was just the power of the subconscious mind and the daily affirmations that made her believe in that particular fact and the universe granted it to her.

In these two stories, there are a few things to note:

1. Siya and Rohan kept repeating affirmations by saying to themselves, they said it again and again to themselves

and the people around them.
2. They both wrote it every day.
3. Siya watched recordings as her mother made some videos, in which she saw a reel of the activities she did. Rohan on the other hand just listened to the audiotapes, to look for his mistakes and to improve on them.

Knowingly or unknowingly, they did the perfect form of affirmations.

In a proper format of practicing affirmation, a person uses:

1. Reading or saying
2. Writing or scripting
3. Listening/seeing

If its not on paper its a vapour, this makes writing the affirmations important.

Affirmations have so much power to influence our subconscious mind that they can do impossible things.

#Tune in the positive affirmations.

CHAPTER NINE

To-do list

You all have 24 hrs in a day. Out of these 24 hours, you sleep 8 hours, on average. One-third of your day goes away, just by sleeping. In other words, you can say, all of us, spend 1/3rd of our life sleeping. You all have only the ⅔ rd in your hand and you should spend it wisely.

If you feel these 16 hours do not suffice your need, and you have to squeeze one or two hours from your sleep, to make yourself more productive. If you think so? You are wrong. Less sleep will keep you lazy and will affect your work efficiency. In order to keep your mind and body in sync adequate sleep is required i.e., 8 hrs. To increase productivity, one has to prioritize all the activities to be done on a particular day. An unplanned day is a wastage as the right priorities are not set.

The world is moving at a very fast pace and to match up the speed, with the fast-moving world, the everyday schedule of each one of us is always hectic. Some days are back-to-back busy with the tasks to be done. The mere thought of many tasks to be done creates chaos in your mind. The mind is juggling and continuously struggling, to do all the tasks. The person slips into a panic zone when this happens. Sometimes, the anxiety to perform so many tasks creates chaos and none of the tasks are done properly. This scenario is very common when a person is multitasking. It drives people crazy, shoots up the blood pressure, sets in the panic attacks, results in anxiety disorder, etc. All this adds up to the mad mind syndrome. The mind fails to work in its full capacity. All these problems popping up can be minimized, just by making a to-do list.

A to-do list provides a schedule as well as the clarity of tasks to be done. Moreover, if you allot dedicated slots for the task to be done at a particular time it makes everything simple and more organized and all chaos and anxiety disappears. To-do lists are a perfect companion when you fail to recognize what to do with your time. A to-do list is the only way to prioritize the activities of your day and make them more purposeful. After doing so, one feels more productive and comfortable by the end of the day.

Maintaining a to-do list also keeps a check to figure out how a person is spending the entire day. The day spent was purposeful or got wasted. This to-do list keeps an eye on your progress.

A To-do list is just like a map that guides you to your destination and is a part of the plan of your journey.

It's not a magic wand but once you develop a habit of doing work according to the to-do list you will explore things that are happening magically. One finds time for almost all the activities one intends to do. The tasks that appeared time taking, gets organized in a shorter span. The time is not wasted in procrastinating rather it is utilized fully to its optimum limit.

Benefits of a to-do list

1. You are more productive.
2 . There is a less chaos in your mind.

3, You have less anxiety.

4. You are more organized.

5. It checks the purposefulness of the day.

It helps in tracking your progress, and what can be tracked can be improved. This to-do list will help you to plan your day in an efficient manner and with proper planning, you will set a habit of doing things in an organized manner leading you towards your goal.

Planning is a crucial part of your journey, if it's planned well it can be executed well. You all are in your journey to make all your dreams and desires to come true , so dont fail to plan your day- to- day life, with the to do list.

There is a famous saying by Benjamin Franklin,

"If you fail to plan, you are planning to fail."

CHAPTER TEN

Habits

Habit means an act, routine, or behaviour that is repeated regularly and it tends to occur subconsciously, without any extra effort later. It can be good or bad. The good habits help you and support you in your journey and make it smooth and make you glide, while the bad ones are like the speed breakers that slow your speed. Anything that has the power to slow down something or helps in speeding up is called the catalyst.

Let's go to your school days to the chemistry lab and recall the experiments you conducted. Adding a few substances to a chemical, used to change the rate of reaction. It sometimes increased its rate and sometimes decreased it, these substances were named catalysts. The catalyst has got the power to change the rate of reaction. Let's make it simpler, with this story.

Rita was a very religious lady, she conducted pooja and havan at her place, every Poornima i.e; on a full moon night. She had a 5 years old grandchild, named Raj, who used to be constantly with her. Raj would stay with her like her shadow. It was Poornima and as usual, the Katha was followed by the havan ritual.

While the process of pooja was on, Raj thought of a mischief and poured a clear liquid kept in the container near the havan- kund, into the havan. That very moment a big fire flared up as the liquid in the container was ghee that was highly inflammable. He got frightened of the big flame and ran away to the other room, some moment later, the priest conducting the pooja sprinkled some clear liquid again along with the mantras, and the fire was controlled, though Raj ran to the adjacent room he was peeping from the door and this seemed to be a magic to him. He wondered how when he poured some clear liquid into the fire, it made the fire flames big, but when the priest sprinkled some other clear liquid, the fire flames were reduced. This question was disturbing him. He waited for the pooja to get over, and the moment the priest left the house after conducting the pooja rituals, he ran to his Grandma and shot his questions one by one.

Raj asked "What was it that I poured into the fire, Grandma and it made the flames big and high? And what magic priest did that made the fire go small again?"

Please, tell me how did it happen, Grandma?

Grandma was amazed by the questions asked by this small wonder. She made him sit and made him understand that he had poured ghee in the fire and the priest had put water in it. Both these substances have different characteristics: one adds to its rate of reaction and the other reduces its rate. The young boy was really young to understand this, so she further added, see you have few friends in your class and some students of your class are not your friends. What do you do when you are with your friend? you talk, play, study, and enjoy. Time passes really fast and you feel happy with that friend, right. The boy said, "yes Grandma". Grandma asked again, "what happens when you sit with a student of your class, whom you don't like at all. You end up in a fight or you quarrel with him and doing your studies seems difficult and it seems that the time is not passing, everything seems boring and is a burden.

Similarly, when fire gets the company of ghee it enjoys its company and does the work fast and big flames are made. On the other hand, when fire gets the company of water it feels boring and full of burden and doesn't work and its flame gets reduced. She further added these substances are called catalysts. The catalyst has the power to increase or decrease the speed of any act. With this small example, Raj understood what Grandma said.

The same is the case with habits, we have some good habits and some bad ones. Good habits are like good friends, and it accelerates our performance with joy. On the other hand, bad habits are like bad friends, and working efficiently in such a company seems difficult. Inculcate good habits and try to get rid of the bad ones as the habits are the catalyst in our growth and performance. If you want to make your dreams, come true and become reality, put in the catalyst of good habits and refrain from the bad ones.

Habits, expedite or slow you, and make you reach the destination on time or delay it.

"Your habits will determine your future." -Jack Canfield

CHAPTER ELEVEN

Happiness is a musk deer

Musk deer is a category of deer found in the Himalayan regions. It is famous for its musk gland, only the male deer has it. Due to the musk gland, it is prone to hunting by the poachers.

The musk deer wanders here and there in search of the fragrance. It runs from one end of the jungle to the other end in search of it. The fragrance for which it is crazy comes from its own musk gland, unaware of the fact, it is busy in search of it. HAPPINESS is also like the musk of the musk deer; it is present in each one of you and you wander from one place to another to find it.

You generalize happiness to be dependent on many things and most of you consider it to be dependent on external factors. The viewpoint regarding happiness differs from person to person. Sometimes you relate it to material things while others attach it to emotional factors. People may have different viewpoints, when you talk about happiness, everyone agrees to accept the fact that it is important to be happy. When asked, what is happiness? Each one of you might have a different answer to it. Happiness is something that cannot be restricted to some constant formula like Force = Mass*Distance.

The perception of happiness is different for each one of you. Happiness is confused with pleasures of life, most of the time, you associate all pleasures with happiness. You equate and attach it to all our likeness but it's not true that likeness is happiness. Happiness is the feeling of contentment within each one of you. It's just like the musk; a musk deer has in it and it fetches that very musk outside without realizing it is inside its body. You must figure out the essence of happiness within you rather than fetching it outside. Finding happiness is more an inward journey rather than an outward one. Start your journey to happiness today. It's just like the musk of the musk deer, very much inside all of you and not outside. Make a habit to stay happy. It gives you a light feeling, a better mental state, helps you do all the tasks with joy in less time. It is a catalyst in the journey of dream, desire and destination.

When you are happy you want to share it and when sad you want to be alone in solitude.

Let's understand it with this story.

Ram had a bad day at work so he was really upset. He had a lovely family but when he returned home after a day's hard work, he was all drained, he asked his wife and daughter to leave him alone. Why alone?

Because he had a bad day. "He was upset, so he requested to leave him alone."

The family was cooperative and wanted to give proper space to Ram to unwind. Days passed and soon Ram resumed his daily routine life, and along with him the family too returned to the same routine. One day in the evening when he came from the office, he was happy and was dancing in joy. Seeing this, his daughter ran to him and he hugged the little girl with joy. The girls asked, " Daddy, why are you so happy today?"

Ram called out his wife's name aloud and added. "Rashmi, come fast, I have great news." Rashmi too got excited and ran towards Ram, she exclaimed, now break the news!

Ram announced it with immense joy. He added, he got a promotion and now he was appointed as a zonal head in his company. His face was shining as the joy reflected on his face. He further added, "darling get ready, let's go out and celebrate."

This was a small story highlighting two different situations,

1. Upset /sad,
2. Happy.

When the situation was sad, he wanted to be alone, on the other hand when he was happy, he wanted to share it with others.

What is the take away in this story?

The nature of happiness is to share, on the other hand, sorrow's nature is to stay aloof in solitude, sorrow is a loner and it's stingy and it refrains from sharing. So, add happiness and share it with the world. Happiness is meant to be shared.

Stay happy to make your journey easy and effortless.

Now that you know happiness is an inside job and its nature is sharing and caring, in the next chapter, I will cover how happiness makes you different from others and the benefits attached with staying happy.

Happiness is an inside job.

CHAPTER TWELVE

Happy vs Unhappy

We often wonder why some people always look happy and some don't. So, let's find what do happy people do and what unhappy people miss?

1. Happy people take responsibility and full accountability for their circumstances; they don't blame others for their failures. The unhappy ones hold other people responsible for every wrong in their life. They have no accountability at all.

2. Happy people live each moment and enjoy the simple joys of life. The unhappy ones keep on waiting for everything to be perfect and time slips away from their hands procrastinating.

3. Happy people are good investors. They invest in their overall wellness. They create an environment of wellness around themselves. The responsibility of personal wellbeing is known to them. They consider life as a gift from God and they thrive to make it better. The unhappy ones find it hard to find time for their own personal wellbeing. They are ignorant of the gift of life given to them.

4. Happy people love themselves; they take steps for their well-being.

Their diet is balanced and they exercise daily to keep fit. The unhappy ones put the blame on others even for not taking care of their body. Isn't it strange?

5. Happy people are always keen to hone new skills. They keep upgrading their skills and knowledge. A happy mind is a curious mind and waits for new information and is open to learning throughout life.

The Unhappy Ones think they know everything and there's no thirst to gain new knowledge or to take up new skills.

6. Happy people are the content ones.

They don't believe in show-offs. They are not comparers nor are obsessed with the symbol of wealth thus they spend money wisely and don't waste money.

The unhappy ones are just the believers of a show-off. They are fond of exhibitions. They are obsessed with symbols of wealth and waste money in showing off unnecessarily. They also compare their lives with others and stay unhappy due to this habit.

7. Happy people are optimistic.

They see opportunities even in small things. They have power-packed enthusiasm for every activity. They are not paralyzed by their fears but they combat fear to win the situation. They see opportunity even in adversity.

The unhappy people are highly pessimistic Even in positive situations they dig out the negativity. They are mentally paralyzed by the fear of losing. Their mindset changes opportunity into an adversity as they refrain from taking any risks.

8. Happy people are thankful and full of gratitude. They practice gratitude every day for the smallest of things they

have in life. The unhappy people don't have gratitude for what they have. The sense of gratitude is missing from their life. They are thankless people. Try to be a happy person as the happy ones are more keen, productive, fit, positive, mentally clear and all this helps in the journey of dream, desire and destination.

Benefits of staying happy.

It opens up the mind and makes you more efficient. A happy mind is a productive mind. It is just like a road without a speed breaker and is like a smooth drive on a highway, it keeps moving you effortlessly towards your goal. A happy mind is more productive because it stays in the present most of the time and focuses on making the present wonderful.

It does not believe in procrastination nor does it live in the past. A happy mind is totally free from the anxieties of the past and the future. It is because of this ability it has no baggage of thoughts for the future or for the past. It is light because it is totally baggage-free.

Have you noticed trucks on the Highway? The loaded trucks cannot run at the high speed because of the load it is carrying. If it tries to speed up, it ends up in an accident mostly because it loses its balance and flips over due to the load it carries. In the same manner, our mind also loses its calm when it's not happy. Stress and anger are the loads that flip the mind and restrict it from functioning in a proper way. Don't be unhappy and create blocks in your life instead stay happy and be free from the load of the past thoughts and of the future.

Drop the baggage if you want speed in life.

If you want to maximize the mind power. You must drop the baggage of all the bad thoughts that occupy your mind. Our mind is just like a computer; all files are saved in memory. But if you save all corrupt files in our system the system will not work properly.

Many of us face the problem of forgetting things even at a young age, this is because our mind is overloaded with corrupt files. The number of corrupt files are more than the important files, which results in difficulty to find Useful files. It is necessary to make our system light by shredding all the corrupt files. Once it is done finding the important files becomes easy.

Life is all about simplification. What has to be in the garbage should be placed in it.

The garbage occupies space, decays after some time to emit a foul smell, attracts bacteria, and results in diseases.

We keep our houses clean from the garbage and dispose of the daily waste. Similarly, we all must dispose of all the garbage of our mind and make it clean and free from the foul smell, bacteria and prevent diseases that can catch our mind. Now let's declutter all that's scattered inside and organize. Once we do it, everything gradually starts falling in place.

A happy mind keeps stress at bay.

Stress is a monster and it elevates the levels of cortisol. Higher cortisol is a catalyst in causing a number of health conditions. The side effect of staying happy is lower cortisol. It's a win-win situation if you are happy. It cuts the chain of further reactions resulting in numerous other diseases. Thus, it is helpful in boosting the immune system.

The research also shows happiness is connected to longevity. If you want to add more years to your life then stay happy.

Now all these things are related, aren't they?

Let's connect the dots,

If you are happy, you live longer. If you are happy, you are more productive. Living a long life with more productivity is a bonus. You live a long life plus you are productive and have a good immune system means less prone to diseases. It's excellent. Isn't it?

It really sounds great. If one decides to stay happy, it's a total win-win situation and you are happy to lose,

What are you going to lose ?

To lose the Stress, the high cortisol, the diseases that arise from the high cortisol, the unproductive behavior, the agony of falling sick.

So, isn't happiness the important thing in your journey of dream, desire and destination

So, when you pack your bags and set yourself on this voyage don't forget to take happiness with you when you travel. It will make your travel more fun, easy, and effortless.

"Happiness is when what you think, what you say and what you do are in a harmony."- Mahatma Gandhi

CHAPTER THIRTEEN

Habits to happiness

Our body and mind together are the vehicle in which our thoughts, desires, and dreams travel. To reach any destination, in which a person travels a distance in between the two points namely the starting point and the finishing point. Whenever you travel in your car to any destination you keep a check on your vehicle. Periodic checking of vehicles is done to refrain from any breakdown in between. Similarly, in this journey of dream desire and destination, I request each one of you to keep a check on yourself so that this journey is swift for you and you travel from your dreams to your destination flawlessly without any breakdown in between. We take care of your vehicle, we get it serviced from time to time, in the same way, every person has to take care of himself, it is very important to keep your body and mind healthy. By doing the following things, you can get a healthy body and mind that will work efficiently and help you reach your destination.

(a) Exercise

Exercise in any form will help you. Did you ever wonder when you go for a walk you feel good or when you exercise you feel good, why does this happen?

You might even find when you walk or exercise your attention and clarity of your mind increases why?

The research shows the human body was designed to walk 12 miles in a day. So, when you do aerobic exercises the heart rate increases resulting in blood flow to increase. Even when you walk the blood flow in the body increases, because of the activity you are doing, the heart pumps more blood and that blood is circulated in different parts of your body including the brain. The brain gets more glucose and oxygen in this process. The blood circulation in the brain also increases resulting in making it more efficient. When the blood circulation is good the body functions better, it mobilizes all the parts of our body, just as the parts of a machine.

The hormone endorphin is released, and as it releases after an exercise, it gives you a feel-good factor. This hormone is particularly a pain killer that is why people with knee pain, back pain, or full-body pain complain less pain when they go for a walk regularly or do some exercises at home. More fitness means more power, more productivity, more positivity, more creativity, and more clarity hence it supports you in your journey of achieving your goals.

"Take care of your body, it's the only place you have to live." - Jim Rohn.

(b) Meditation

Meditation is getting your brain trained to be focused more and to redirect your thoughts. It's putting yourself in sync with your surroundings. For me, writing with my full awareness is meditation, for my grandma, it's her worship time and for my aunt it's gardening.

Now, the question arises, what is meditation?

The meaning of meditation is to concentrate the mind to any one subject by holding it.

Meditation is a word that has gained so much popularity because of its benefits, but the heaviness of the word itself creates a fear in trying it. There are major misconceptions related to it, as it's time-consuming, difficult to get a grip of it, etc but the moment you try it for as minimum as 10 minutes daily, you notice incredible changes in yourself. These changes come slowly to you with your consistent practice.

Meditation is something that can be experienced and can't be put down in words. Meditation brings just your conscious awareness in sync with the present. You breathe and you are not conscious about it, just the focus on breathing makes it a conscious process and turns the very effect into meditation. Meditation puts down all the walls that you have built around yourself with a conditioned mind and gives you a brand-new chance to open new doors by putting those barriers down.

The more you meditate you bring your inside and outside in sync and find a better you. With meditation, your mind calms down and a calm mind is a better state of mind when it comes to work

What calmness of mind does, let's understand through this short story.

A village boy was sitting near a pond. He was thinking something. While thinking he saw his reflection and got scared as he was engrossed in his thoughts. He was thinking about his future as he had just passed his tenth grade. He was good at studies but had no money to pursue further education, he belonged to a very poor family of blacksmiths and his family somehow managed their livelihood with difficulty, having three meals was also a hassle, so arranging money for education was out of the question. He was all grown up according to his dad, and his dad was looking at his son as an earning hand, but the son had dreams to pursue and continue his education. This worry and anxiety had left him imbalanced and fury was built in his mind. He had hatred and anger for his father and wondered why he was born in such a family where affording food three times also sounded like having a luxury.

He was boiling inside and failed to find a solution to his question. He was angry and frustrated and both these things had brought him to the pond as he wanted to end his life. He was angry and was thinking of ending his life and was also thinking about what will happen after he takes this step. While thinking he picked up pebbles and threw them into the pond at the point where he saw his reflection a moment back. As soon as he threw the pebble, he could not find his reflection instead ripples were formed on the water surface, he kept on throwing pebbles one after the other and tried to see his reflection but he failed, he got tired throwing pebbles and looking for his reflection but all he could find was the ripples formed after throwing the pebbles.

He sat down for a while and closed his eyes and remembered all the good things that had happened in his life. He was revisiting his childhood days with his parents for the last time and was gathering the courage to jump into the pond to end his life. He opened his eyes and was about to jump and what he saw was his reflection in the water again, he paused for a moment and sat down again.He sat and wondered what magic had happened, a few moments back he was struggling to find his reflection and again it was back. He recollected that the still water is showing the reflection but when the pebbles are thrown into it, it fails to show the reflection. He halted and realized his mind was unstable as it was filled with anger, frustration, and anxiety and was unable to find the solution.

Now he closed his eyes again and started taking long breaths, all he was doing was just breathing and he focused on it for 10 mins. He felt better, his anxiety, fear were all gone and an idea of studying in the school in the second shift clicked his mind. He decided to continue his education while working with his father. With a calm mind, he thought and was able to find a solution to his question. He was able to do this because he understood that the mind was like the water of the pond, the reflection disappeared when the stone was thrown into the water and as soon as it became stable, the ripples disappeared and his reflection appeared again.

"The calmness of mind is the beautiful jewels of wisdom", as mentioned by James Allen in his book, "As a man thinketh." In this book, the benefits of calmness are mentioned and covered in a very appropriate manner. He mentions beautifully, ***"a calm mind is like a shade-giving tree in a thirsty land or a sheltering rock in a storm."***

In this journey of your dreams, calmness of mind will play a key role as this journey will be a roller coaster ride for you. You will love the highs but the lows will shatter you, it will be a mixture of achievements and failures, it might happen you have to start again and again. There will be unanticipated problems and the strength to handle all the problems will come from a calm mind that is only possible through meditation. Enjoy your journey with full vigor and adopt the mantra of calmness to handle all the challenges on the way.

"The more tranquil a man becomes, the greater is his success, his influence, his power to good. The calmness of mind is one of the beautiful jewels of wisdom."- James Allen

(c) Food and nutrition

Food and nutrition are the vital components needed for the proper functioning of our bodies. Proper food in the form of a balanced diet is needed to keep the body functional. Eating good food in adequate quantity keeps you healthy and free from illness and diseases. Hence, it boosts immunity. A better immunity keeps you fit and functional in the long run. If you take proper care of your food and nutrition it makes you happy and the moment this equilibrium is disturbed, the behavior of a person changes.

The most common example of the effect of food deprivation is visible in a child. When there is a delay in feeding the baby, the baby gets cranky, starts crying, throws tantrums. This also happens in adults when the chain of proper food nutrition is not maintained you may witness mood swings and irritation. All this comes into action due to the hormone dopamine also known as the reward hormone, it is released after eating food that uplifts the mood leaving you with a great sense of joy.

Follow a set time to have your breakfast, lunch, and dinner. When you are fit and healthy you work consistently towards your goals hence reaching your dream destination becomes easy.

Your body is also a vehicle and you have to put in the fuel as food and water to keep it running in a very good state.

"One cannot think well, love well, sleep well if one has not dined well."- Virginia Wolf

(d) Take an early shower daily and get ready.

We take shower daily as it helps us to feel fresh and active. The time of shower is important, some people prefer to take shower before they sleep, some in the evening, and some in the morning. The purpose of a shower is to keep the body clean and fresh as thought by many people. But it's not just to keep your body fresh and clean, it has many other benefits attached and you might be unaware of it.

The time of shower has its effect on the body. The shower before sleep calms you down and helps in giving you a sound sleep on the other hand when it's taken early in the morning it has many benefits,

1. It helps you start your day early with an added dose of freshness.
2. It washes away toxins from your body.
3. It improves blood circulation, resulting in calming down your anxiety and blood pressure.
4. It enhances positive mood, when you start the day with a positive mood it pools more positivity.

5. It enhances the creative flow of your brain.

6. With calmness, positivity, and creative flow you tend to be more productive and efficient.

This shower is just like cleaning your house and putting the garbage outside your house as you do every day. If you leave your house dirty and the garbage in the house it will attract flies and bacteria. The same happens with your body the moment you take an early morning shower, you are fresh and clean in all aspects mental as well as physical. No one has stopped you from taking a second shower take it when you need but do make sure you take an early morning shower.

Get dressed every day after an early shower, don't spend half of the day in your sleepwear. Getting ready has its benefits and if you do it early in the morning, nothing like it.

This habit will help you to extract the best throughout your day.

India is a country of culture and traditions. Here, we have this habit of starting the day with a bath and getting dressed. This wisdom is hidden in the chaupai of Hanuman Chalisa. Hanuman Chalisa is a compilation of 40 chaupai that has lots and lots of hidden wisdom in it.

Hanuman Chalisa has a chaupai highlighting the importance of getting ready/ dressed as soon as you start your day.

It says "Kanchan baran biraj subesa
Kanan kundal kunchit kesaa ."

This means, your body is as shiny as gold, and you put on good attires on it, you wear studs in your ears as ornaments and your hair is neatly done.

In today's era, your progress depends on how well-groomed and presentable you are. If you have the right talents but you are not presentable it will affect your career graph. Your personality should be pleasing as well as presentable to get success in life.

This wisdom is right from the age of saints and sages who are following it and reaping the benefits. In the modern era too presentability matters a lot. You have won half the battle, if you are well dressed and presentable.

Adapt the habit of bathing early and get ready to reap its benefit in your life.

"Life is a party , dress for it.'- Audrey Hepburn

(e) Sleep

Sleep is often not considered a vital factor in happiness and this is the biggest mistake one makes. Some people compromise on sleep without knowing the repercussions it can cause and that can be fatal. Don't make this mistake of compromising on your sleep. Proper sleep of eight hours is important. Not having proper sleep puts our system in chaos; it fails to function to its optimum capacity. Sleep is the maintenance hours your body needs. All the cleaning, repair, and energy refueling take place when you sleep and when you cut short your sleep hours this repair, cleaning, and refueling is disrupted.

Let's understand this with a story

Rahul and Ruchi went on a vacation to Dubai from India. They took a night flight, they reached Dubai in the early hours and reached the reception of the hotel they had booked. Though they reached the destination, the hotel rooms were not alloted as it was, 8 AM and regular check-in timings were 10 AM onwards. They knew the guest had already left the room but still, they had to wait for two hours before checking in. When they inquired at the reception, the manager said, the guest had already checked out but as a protocol, they have to clean and maintain the room so that it's ready and fresh for the next guest. Out of curiosity, Rahul asked what they do, which takes as long as two hours.

The reception manager told him that deep cleaning of the room and bathroom with the disinfectant is done to make sure no inconvenience to the next guest is caused. The supplies of water, toiletries, and other basic commodities are checked to ensure the comfortable stay of the guest. The room is made ready and fresheners are sprayed to enhance the freshness of the room so that the guest who arrives gets no clue of who had stayed in this room earlier. It's clean and fresh that adds to the vibes of the guest who checks in the room.

While giving all this description the time passed and it was time for the lovely couple to check in their allotted room. They checked in the room allotted and enjoyed the fresh vibes and this made their stay happy and memorable.

This is what happens to your body when you sleep. The body refuels and repairs itself and gets ready for the next day.

You all live in your body first, so take care of it and help it in its proper functioning, so that it functions properly and runs for a longer time. Sleep more to dream more.

"O sleep! O gentle sleep! Nature's soft nurse."- William Shakespeare

(f) Expose yourself to nature.

Nature in itself is abundant, whatever we crave is available in nature and because of this very trait, it is called mother nature. Exposing yourself to the flora and fauna of nature brings a sense of joy. If you stay indoors to avoid the sun and fresh air, after some time you start feeling low, and depressed. When you expose yourself to nature, you are in better sync with your surroundings. When it is done serotonin is released, the hormone responsible for stabilizing mood.

Few activities which release this hormone are sun exposure, mindfulness, nature exposure, meditation. It is only when you are in a good mood you are creative and efficient and if it is not the case there is room for irritation and destructive thoughts. When you are in a good mood you are willing to do the chores you hate. You work with full zeal in a good mood, but when the bad mood cycle comes, the task you love seems to be a burden. You fuss and fume and spoil your peace and happiness.

Let's understand with this story.

Aanya was a computer engineer and used to be very busy with her work. She hardly found time to go on trips and vacations but she used to go on morning walks and then used to spend her full day in the office. Cooking for herself also seemed to be a big burden to her so she preferred to order her food from outside. Her friend Natasha flew down from the US to meet her and she had a gluten allergy that made her incompetent to eat the food from outside. Natasha told this to Aanya that it would be impossible for her to eat outside and only if Aanya finds it comfortable to cook for her then only, she would come to meet her. Aanya was excited and full of joy when she heard that Natasha, who has been her friend since childhood, was planning to meet her.

The joy of meeting a friend, a buddy made her forget her shortcomings. Aanya knew that she hated to cook but because she was in a good mood, she committed to cook for her joyfully. All this happened because of her joyful mood. Natasha came to her place for three days. Both of them had a great time together. Gradually as days passed, Aanya got busy with her office work and the same cycle of ordering food resumed. She also stopped going on walks. She stayed indoors due to her work commitments. One fine Sunday her neighbour next door Nisha, whom Aanya liked from the core of her heart, rang the bell.

Aanya had an ongoing project and it was causing lots of stress in her life, she was in a bad mood, her neighbour Nisha just asked for a bowl of sugar. Since Aanya was under stress and not in a good mood, she misbehaved with her neighbour who had helped her many times in the past. Though Aanya didn't intend to do so, because of work pressure and scolding from her seniors, she was in a terrible mood and she misbehaved. After a few days when her project was over and the work pressure was at bay, she realized that she misbehaved with her neighbour and it was not right. This behavior created a drift in their relationship.

A hand that was always available to help her was mistreated and Nisha had now built a distance from her.

Aanya again started her walks in the morning, then she realized her mistake. Later Aanya apologized to Nisha for her behavior and made things work for them, just like before. The mood builds and breaks relations. It is necessary to check your mood. A mood changes with a nature walk and makes difficult things simple due to enhanced creativity. Mood plays a vital role. A good mood makes you creative and bad makes you destructive.

Check your mood while you are in this journey of dream, desire and destination as your good mood will enhance your creativity and efficiency and will help you, while the bad mood will pull you back and will make you do destructive things that may retard your progress in this journey making the destination seem far for you.

The outdoor walk, in the sun, stabilizes mood, the socializing while walking in the park helps in releasing the oxytocin hormones that helps in uplifting your mood, going regularly on a walk sets a disciplined routine and gives a feeling of accomplishing a task and completing a goal that helps in the release of dopamine that is a reward chemical released after hitting a goal and self-care or eating good food. So now connect the dots and see the advantages of being active and exposing yourself to nature. One good habit pulls in the second and so on. It creates a chain of positivity.

"In every walk with nature, one receives far more than he seeks."- John Muir

CHAPTER FOURTEEN

Invest in yourself

The best investment ever is to invest in yourself. The best outcome you get is after this investment. Your body is an entity. As you live in a house your soul lives in your body. The mind lives in your body and similarly, for all the organs your body is the home. Whatever you put inside has its effect. If you eat well, you will get healthy and strong, if you indulge in bad eating and drinking habits it will make you unhealthy. If you exercise daily, you will train your muscles hence, they will grow strong. If you don't, it becomes fragile and weak. Similarly, if you put in efforts to develop your skills, you will learn and earn wisdom and later you earn money from that skill and wisdom. The moment you decide to invest in yourself in grooming and sharpening your skills, gradually you step towards the growth mindset.

The people who have a growth mindset find and try to find different ways to grow themselves in all the spheres of life. They thrive hard to improve themselves in all aspects of life, to be successful. They are different from people who have a fixed mindset who are restricted to what they know and don't have an eagerness to learn new things. These people are not open to changes, so they avoid changes, as an output, they remain the same throughout many years, and in doing so they fail to tap into new opportunities, as they lack those skills. The world is changing at a very fast pace, if you fail to adapt to the growth mindset you miss many things, so upgrade yourself with the skills to match up with the age in which you are living, and welcome changes and more new opportunities and match your footsteps with the fast-moving world.

People with a growth mindset believe in investing in themselves to reap more from life. Anything you invest in, let's say for e.g.: reading, gives you many benefits. It helps in improving your concentration, sets a discipline, improves your life as you read you gain from the knowledge put in the form of writing.

The growth mindset gives you the room for development on yourself and it happens by investing in yourself. It diminishes the fear of trying new things because of your skill sets and abilities hence providing you the potential to achieve anything you desire or dreamt of.

In this Journey of dream, desire and destination pledge to invest in yourself and adopt a growth mindset, so that you can throw yourself into the pool of opportunities and can reach your destination with ease as you have the proper tools to do so with the investment you have made on yourself.

"The best investment you can make is an investment in yourself. The more you learn, the more you will earn."- Warren Buffett

CHAPTER FIFTEEN

Fear and faith

Fear and faith both have a common friend, belief.

You all have friends; friendship is the relationship that you relish the most. You all laugh, giggle, play and have fun in your friend's company. It happens sometimes that the person with whom you are friends are also friends with other people. In this process, you discover common friends and then later end up becoming friends with them, only if you share similar choices in life otherwise you find it difficult to gel with them. You might not be friends with them but your common friend continues to be friends with such a person. I hope many of you must have experienced this situation.

A common friend is common for you and that person whom you don't know. Just like you, fear and faith too have a common friend in their life. Yes, you heard it right like you and me the faith and fear have a common friend named belief. Faith and belief are very good friends and so are belief and fear. Faith loves light and fear loves darkness. But faith and fear hate each other and don't want to stay in the same room, where there is faith, the fear goes away, and when fear stays faith goes away. When belief comes with faith, they both become so happy and in happiness, they want to climb the stairs and keeps climbing the stairs one by one. It happens because belief in faith's company feels the light that is why it climbs the stairs fast and it keeps doing it as faith loves light and in search of light, both climbs up and up and reaches the heights.

Similarly, the fear too has belief as a friend, but in its company, beleif becomes lazy and heavy, it finds climbing stairs a difficult task to do, so it chooses to get down, as fear likes darkness, it goes in the direction opposite to the light, it gets one step down and down and keeps going down in search of darkness and keeps going deeper and deeper in search of darkness. This brings fear and belief to the deepest and the darkest place.

Here, faith and fear both had belief as a common friend in whose company two different results were achieved. One led towards the light and reached the heights by going up and up and the other reached the depth of darkness by going deeper and deeper.

What will you choose?

Faith with belief or fear with belief!

Faith also has three big rivals and these are doubt, fear, and incapacity of decision making. These three things give fear more strength and it defeats faith easily and effortlessly.

So, replace fear, doubt, and indecisiveness with faith, courage, and decision.

Let your faith win over all your fears. If you are successful in defeating all your fears, you are successful in crossing the hurdles in the journey of your dreams and desires and would finally reach the finishing point of your destination.

"Fear is faith in reverse gear."- Napoleon Hill

"One can become whatever one wants to be, if one constantly contemplates on the object of desire with faith."- Shrimad Bhagavad Gita

CHAPTER SIXTEEN

Choose your company wisely

Less is more, apply this principle when it comes to friendship.

Choose your friends and the company of people wisely. Don't hesitate to disconnect the wire of such friendship, and people who are disguised as friends and are no more adding value to your life. Friends come in different shapes and sizes. Some friends are just a time pass, they only remember you in their leisure time or when they are free. They are never available when you need them. In the modern era, the idea behind friendship has changed. The primary requirement of friendship is not emotional support rather it is for mutual benefit. Friendship in the modern era is mostly for clubbing, partying, networking, travelling, business, etc. There is always a secret purpose hidden behind such friendships.

Some friends are disguised as friends but are not real friends at all. They are just interested in peeking into your life and your daily happenings, their main aim is to keep an eye on your lifestyle. Stay away from such friends, who kill your precious time gossiping and are the gossip queens and the kings. All they have, is to talk about the negative attributes of others. Friendships are basically for some gain by one person or the other. In very rare cases the friendship is pure. Look for the friends who want to be your friend without benefits. The friendship should be selfless and unconditional, both of you must learn from each other, being friends.

When you are in the company of so-called friends who are not true friends at all, just keep a check on your vibrations after meeting such people. Is there a boost in your energy level or is there a depreciation in your energy level? If you get a boost after meeting such friends then the friendship has passed the litmus test and such a friend gives you positivity but in case of such people whom you meet or talk to and you feel deprived of energy, such a person drains your precious time and energy by talking negative stuffs. Such talks and interactions are worthless and add no value at all.

It is asserted, you are the average of five people in whose company you live. Choose those sets of five people, very cautiously. If you have five positive people around you, your energy levels will get a boost, if not it will be quite draining.

Understand it with an example.

Can you charge anything with a discharged battery? Of course not.

Those negative people are imprisoned by negativity and are discharged; they have nothing left except negativity; all they can give you is the negative vibes. Whatever comes in their contact is engulfed into the pool of negativity. Staying away from them is advisable.

A nice battery when placed along with the discharged battery never works. If you want to get charged, get yourself connected to the one with a full charge.

Remember, you can withdraw funds from an account that has money in it, an account with no money will hand you over, the receipt mentioning "insufficient funds."

Cut your friend circle short. Simplify it without hesitation. Keep only those who add value to your life and make you feel uplifted. Shred all others like a waste paper, they occupy unnecessary space in your mind and life amounting to your mental agony. Set yourself free from the captivity of such friends. Hold on to the positive people and trash down those who don't fit to add any value to your life. Setting yourself free from this burden is very important. Use your time wisely by putting inputs to improve your own life rather than wasting time with negative people. Once this baggage is dropped, you move on to the new dimensions of your well-being. This helps you to align yourself to more joy and happy self as the focus on your own life will add more to your well-being. Drop the guilt and outgrow such people and open new doors to add more value to your own life.

Let me tell you a fact, iron as a substance gets converted into a totally different substance when it comes in contact with oxygen, and it has a different result when it comes in contact with carbon. The iron when it comes in contact with the carbon, do you know what changes it undergoes, to your surprise these two combines to form steel. Steel, as you all know, is known for its strength and durability. On the other hand, when the same iron comes in contact with oxygen, it combines to form rust. Rust as you all know eats up and erodes the main substance iron, and hence after some time, rust makes the substance weak and non-durable. Rust makes it hollow and weak.

So, choose your company wisely, check what kind of people you are surrounded with. If you are among the learned people, you will gain knowledge and wisdom, if you are among the thieves, you will pick the habit of stealing. Company has a huge impact on the human mind. Check your company and change your destiny.

Henry Ford is another example, he began his career and had poverty, illiteracy, and ignorance around him but within the short period of ten years, he overcame all these things just by the right company. His life changed when he became the personal friend of Thomas. A. Edison. He had also formed acquaintances with great men namely Harvey Firestone, John Burroughs, and Luther Burbank, all these men had great brains, within mere a period of 25 years, he overcame poverty, illiteracy, and ignorance and was in the right company of great men with brains and because of this, he was able to become one of the richest men in America.

Company of person or association of any person with anyone results in the exchange of energy, the importance of association is beautifully explained by Vivekananda through these lines.

Explaining the meaning of "Association" he said, the raindrops from the sky: if it is caught in the hands, it's pure enough for drinking if it falls in a gutter, its value drops so much that it can't be used even for washing the feet. If it falls on a hot surface, it perishes. If it falls on a lotus leaf, it shines like a pearl and finally, if it falls on an oyster, it becomes a pearl. The drop is the same, but its existence and worth depend upon with whom it associates.

Always be associated with people who are good at heart. Check the company of people you live with and spend your precious time wisely.

"You are the average of the five people you spend the most time with."-Jim Rohn

" Show me your friends and I will tell you who you are."-Vladimir Lenin.

CHAPTER SEVENTEEN

Power of thoughts

The thought makes a person powerful or powerless, happy or sad, good or bad. The mad mind is not mad indeed. It's mad due to its incapacity to work properly, stress and anxiety adds to it. But from where does this stress and anxiety comes? It all comes from our minds. First, it is a thought that later becomes anxiety or stress.

The type of thought you have is based on the event that happens in your life. Then comes your interpretation of thoughts that is dependent on your self-beliefs. Next comes the outcome or the consequence of the act. The consequence of the act results in the emission of your emotions, happiness, sad, angry, etc

The mind is a good slave but a bad master, if you leave on the mind to analyse and interpret everything, it will try to master you. In such a case there is a gap between your thoughts and what is going around. When the alignment of that very moment differs from what is pre-decided by the mind, in such a disagreement there is a ruckus created between the two and the mind starts its show. It shouts, screams, and creates all drama just to set the alignment that it wants. You witness a continuous dance of light and shadow juggling to set in the alignment.

If shouting, screaming win over the surrounding, all that is around bows down to the drama, and the mad mind wins and creates all more drama each passing day. But when the surrounding refuses to align to the thoughts of the furious mind and it fails and has to stop the ongoing show.

The furious mind in such a case has no other option other than calming down and stopping screaming and shouting. Now you have control over your mind, so direct your mind in a positive direction to have a positive mindset and a positive direction.

Find the clarity of what you want? This question is of prime importance. What you want or desire must be clear.

This desire ignites inside you and is mainly triggered by your dreams mostly i.e., what you actually aspire to achieve in life. Identifying what you really want. It gives you a direction to work on that very purpose and you take steps to achieve those goals. Now next comes, how do you feel just thinking about it? If it is achieved, if this thought gives you pleasure, you start taking action for it else if it doesn't excite you much, you drop the action steps to be followed.

The clarity of what you want is really very critical, deciding this very fact sets you on the voyage to take steps to grab them with your actions. Next comes action, Thomas Alva Edison has said, if you want different results then you must change your actions as the same action will always fetch you the same result.

In order to achieve your dreams or desires, you must change what you are doing for ages. Otherwise, these same actions will lead to the same results that you have always got for many years. So, when you want to do something new, your action steps must be new and different from what you have been doing in your past.

Every action has an equal and opposite reaction, so mind your actions as actions are highly associated with feelings of you. Feeling good about it gives you a push, even if you feel bad and want that bad feeling to change into a good one, you need to take actions. Only actions have the power to change pain into pleasure or pleasure to pain.

Let's understand it with an example.

Radha is an obese girl and she feels bad about her weight. She really feels embarrassed of her heavy body so a great pain is associated with her body image. Only her actions have the power to change this pain into pleasure. Now she decides to keep a check on her weight and takes actions to change the feeling to pleasure by losing weight.

The action will include a diet chart to keep calorie check and exercise to lose fat. With these consistent actions, she will achieve what she desires and can reach her destination, and will gradually change the feeling from pain to pleasure. The thoughts you have determine your mindset.

If you have more positive thoughts you are dominated by positive thoughts and positivity will reflect in our behaviour. If you are positive only for a small span and you jump back to the negativities your behaviour will reflect negativity. In this journey, hold your thinking firmly, because you will reach your dream destination only if your thinking is determined to achieve your dreams.

"The greatest discovery of my generation is that human beings can alter their lives by altering their attitude of mind:" as you think, so shall you be." -William James

"We are addicted to our thoughts. We cannot change anything if we don't change our thinking."-Santosh Kalwar

"The soul becomes dyed with the colour of its thoughts"-Marcus Aurelies

CHAPTER EIGHTEEN

Deserve then desire

Desire is a wish, and dreams can't exist if there are no desires. You can say that desire is the fire that ignites the dream. In this journey of dream, desire, and destination the desire of doing something must compulsorily be a burning one. If it's not a burning desire, achieving dreams becomes tough.

Each one of you are like a vehicle with a sufficient amount of fuel, but you all are unaware of the fact that you have the fuel inside you, only those who have a burning desire of achieving something works on , putting the ignition of the vehicle on. Now, the vehicle starts and it covers small distances every day. While the other vehicles remain at the starting point because it was never given the ignition as the desire to drive the vehicle was missing. On the other hand, the one with the burning desire couldn't wait and took action to fulfil the desire by giving the ignition to the vehicle and it covered small distances every day.

Now, when this vehicle has travelled a significant distance and is now looked upon by the other vehicles, they think it's magic, but it's the effort of the burning desire that pushed it to take that action and risk and because of those actions taken this vehicle, is now ahead of others.Check yourself and put your ignition on, if you want to reach your destination or keep waiting at the starting point. You don't lack the fuel, you lack ignition i.e., action.

I would like to share a story that my grandfather always narrated to me, when I was a child. He used to say desires are unlimited and it's not possible to fulfil all of them and it's not justified to keep many desires, be choosy in your desires and make yourself deserving for that desire. What he meant to say was it's not enough to have desires, one must make oneself fit to deserve what that person is aiming to desire in life.

He further added that in the village there was a boy who was very lean and thin and he desired to become a bodybuilder, all villagers used to laugh at him, seeing his malnourished body and made fun of him. He used to feel really bad about it, the fun was made because he was desiring something that he didn't deserve, this is what the villagers thought. But that lean and thin boy had a burning desire to fulfil his dream and he started working towards it slowly, and made himself deserving to achieve that very goal of becoming a bodybuilder.

What changed suddenly that made him deserving was, the inputs he made to achieve his goal. He started working out and increased his diet in order to do so. Without taking this action, he was not fit for the deserving category. He took actions to achieve his desires that was indeed a burning one and that made him deserving.

Now, the question arises, what makes you deserving, my grandfather asked me?

I failed to answer this question at that time as I was very young, but now when I recapitulate this story, I easily figure out that it's our actions that makes us deserving of the desire to be conquered.

We all have the oil and the wick in the lamp, only the action to light it up is required. So, just keeping a desire in the heart is not enough. You have to be an action taker and keep doing the consistent efforts to achieve all your desires and dreams.

There is a proverb, "first deserve then desire", it means, prove worthy of yourself by working hard consistently.

Be consistent in your actions.

Small actions when repeated for a very long time, give great results.

Let's understand with this example.

Any person who intends to do a weight loss goes to the gym or on the walk daily, if you walk for two days and hope to see the result you will be disappointed on the other hand if you are consistently working out for 6 months and show your persistence and hard work in fulfilment of your desire you will surely see the result. It may take time, but yes, it will show you the result. If you take proper actions and make yourself deserving for the fulfilment of that goal or desire one day it becomes a reality.

Napoleon Hill has mentioned in his book, "Think and grow rich the principle of stickability and quitability. It mentions that those who stick to a plan and are persistent and don't quit are successful. He wonderfully curated and narrated the story of the uncle of his friend R U Darby and his stickability lesson in selling the insurance which he learned from the quitability in gold mining.

Darby along with his uncle was caught in the "gold fever" and they went to Colorado to dig gold and grow rich. They mined the gold ore and shipped it to a smelter. They had good profits, later they realized that the reserves were over and were bringing no more profits. They drilled to some distance and gave up, as they thought it was not bringing in the profits to them. Finally, they had quit mining without seeking proper expert opinion and took the train back home. After quitting the machinery was sold to the junkman for a few hundred dollars, who called in a mining engineer to look at the mine and do little calculating. The engineer found the project had failed because the owners were not familiar with the fault lines. His calculations showed the vein would be found just three feet away from where Darby had stopped drilling. And that was where the gold was found, the junkman took millions of dollars from the mine because he knew to seek expert counsel, before giving up.

It's clear enough to say, if Darby had stuck to drilling for three feet more, he would have discovered it and made huge profits out of it. From this, Darby adapted the stickability principle, and refused to quit while selling the insurance that was his newly chosen field. He said to himself "I stopped three feet away from gold, but will never stop when men say "no" when I ask them to buy insurance."

Later, he made huge profits by selling insurance by adapting the stickability principle, which he learned after quitability in gold mining. He was one of the small group of men who sold millions of dollars in life insurance annually and became rich.

This story gives a strong lesson to go on and on and never quit. If you have a desire, stick to it and keep working on it persistently and never quit.

Your body is the vehicle in which your dreams and desires travel and it's your duty to put in all the efforts in the form of fuel to help the vehicle reach its destination.

"Believe in stickability, not in quitability."

CHAPTER NINETEEN

Techniques

Some techniques that will help you to reprogram your mind.

Envelope exercise

Let's begin with the envelope technique. It's quite easy and simple, just grab an envelope and write your postal address on it. Now, without any delay, write a letter to yourself and write down the most intricate details of your dreams and desires and write it with a perspective as you have already achieved it. Mention how you wanted this to happen and how much joy you are feeling after fulfilling it. Write it with all your emotions and if you really do so, you will be amazed to read it, when it's delivered to you.

Yes, write it and post it to yourself. Don't miss it.

If there is any problem with posting, you can drop it in your letterbox and collect it after three days.

I am sure you will be really delighted to read this letter to yourself and will experience another level of joy.

Once you receive it, do read this letter daily for 21 days without fail.

Why read it for 21 days?

It's to change your neural pattern. It will tune your mind in 21 days and will make you believe in what is written in the letter. You can keep it in such a place that you can see it daily or you can paste it on your vision board too or simply fold it and keep it in your pocket. Every time you will put your hands in your pocket you will touch it and you will get a signal in your mind that will remind you of the feeling. Once you feel it, you will start to vibrate at that frequency and very soon you will attract all what your desire.

Everything around us is in the form of vibrations and frequency and like stuffs attracts other stuffs that vibrates at that frequency. Happiness vibrates at a greater frequency so it attracts joy and success along with it, sadness vibrates at a low frequency so it attracts sorrow and misery along.

This technique was adopted by Bruce lee to achieve his dream of becoming a successful actor. This sense of joy will attract more joys in the future for sure. By now you know the habits of happiness and what happiness does to you as it's mentioned in the previous chapters. Keep the pool of positivity intact around you to raise your vibrations.

Afformations

Do your affirmations daily. Read, write and listen to your affirmations. The importance of affirmation is also covered in the affirmation chapter before, here I will highlight another level of it that is called afformation.

Yes, it's not a spelling mistake, it's a term called "AFFORMATION."

The affirmation is the affirmative statement that we say every day and want our mind to believe, it's true, it helps to tap the subconscious mind. The human mind likes throwing questions, and in this process, the mind asks, why are you making such statements? you don't believe it. Here begins the role of afformations when the why is answered. The moment you answer the why attached to your affirmation it produces feelings that are again energy and it gives you the motivation to take actions for that empowering question. The answers you give produce the feeling of immense self-worth and push you to take action.

If you dive deep into it to understand, it is driven by two components: the why and the how. The why covers the area, what's your intention for doing it, and the how covers the action steps involved. While doing affirmation you say, I am healthy and while doing afformation you ask, Why am I so healthy and list your answers in support of it.

Noah St. John birthed this idea after experiencing great resistance and disbelief while saying affirmations. With this the affirmations that seemed fruitless became fruitful and impactful.

Practice the afformations with your affirmations to get results.

The water technique

The water technique is one of the important techniques to reprogram your subconscious mind.

Water as you all know is the universal solvent and has the power to dissolve everything in it. If you put salt, it will dissolve salt in it, if you put sugar, it will dissolve sugar. Even the hardest metal put into it will dissolve in it, might be its quantity is very less, but it will dissolve.

So, what do you have to do? You have to take a crystal glass and fill it with water and put all our intentions into the glass of water by reading the goal card you have made or the letter you wrote to yourself.

Just put the card in such a place and hold the water in your hand and read it at least three times. Remember to put all your emotions in your words and hold the glass with both hands so that the major surface of the glass is covered with your palm.

It's strange, but to your surprise, it's not a small act, you are transferring all your energy, as I have earlier mentioned and by now you all know that everything around us is in the form of energy and it has frequencies and vibrations.

So, once the repetition is complete, at least keep doing till three repetitions then you drink the water slowly with full faith thinking that all your dreams and desires are coming true. The best time to do this activity is in the morning after you get up and at night before you sleep. Do this act at least for five days continuously and see your dreams and desires shaping up to reality. This water technique is very effective as it has science in it. The research has proved that the water has memory in it.

One of the most prevalent experiments was done by the Japanese researcher Dr. Masaru Emoto and was recorded in his book " The message from water." The study proved how vibrational energy has an impact on water.

Three bowls of water were kept in different environments and were tested.

The first bowl was placed in the room in which a happy couple lived and had immense love for each other. All they had was love and only love. So, the aura of the room was full of energy of love and when the bowl was kept there, it also vibrated with the same frequencies and vibrations.

The second bowl was kept in a room in which an angry couple lived and fought over the petty issues.

The couple picked up fights for any petty issue and kept on fighting continuously, so the environment of that room was full of negative vibes of the fight and when the bowl full of water was kept in that room, it had similar energies transferred into it.

The third bowl was kept in the room of an old couple who were religious. They sang religious songs and recited shlokas from the religious books. That room had an environment of spirituality around them. The room had spiritual energy all around and was full of peace and serenity and that energy got transferred to the water in the bowl.

Now, all the bowls molecular patterns were observed and the picture of the molecular structures were taken. It showed that water arranged it in different crystalline structures depending on the stimulus given to it.

In this experiment, the water was kept in a different environment to test the effect of the environment on the water. The observations were very surprising. The bowls of the lovey-dovey couple and the religious couple created beautiful geometric patterns as harmonious emotions such as love, appreciation, peace and serenity were transferred while the one kept in the room of the fighting couple had harsher emotions transferred as a result it created the fragmented patterns. This example in itself, is the greatest proof to support that the energy gets transferred to the water.

The water technique works because of this memory property of water in it, when you hold a glass full of water in your palm and set your intentions and repeat those for five times, the energy gets transferred into the water and when you drink it, you transfer that energy inside you and it gets transferred to each cell of your body. The human body has 70 percent water, and our cell too has water in it, as a result it quickly starts showing resonance and the magic begins.

Take a note that what started outside in a glass of water is now inside your body and it carries all the intentions that you have put into it. Be very careful about putting your intentions, what you will put will reach inside and multiply.

Many people around the globe are using this technique to fulfil their desires and have benefited with it. There are records to prove people have cured diseases, achieved success and many other things with this technique. This is the technique to be used free of cost, all you need is a glass and water to fill it, that's it. Go, give it a try, and change your life miraculously.

Remember to do it early in the morning after doing your affirmations and at night before you go to sleep for at least five days. You can continue doing this for 21 days for greater benefits, as you know in order to reprogram your mind and to change the neural pattern it must be done for 21 days.

Water technique steps

Step 1: Grab a glass of water, in a glass made of glass or crystal.

Step 2: Set all your positive intentions of your desire, that you want to achieve.

Step3: Repeat it three times, repeat with full emotions, express your happiness, while holding the glass as you desire is fulfilled, let the positive energy flow.

Step 4: Now, look into the glass and affirm that it has all the positive vibes in it that you have just said and drink it slowly.

Step 5: While drinking it, feel as if all positive energy is transferred inside and you are full of all those energies that you have just thrown into the water.

Step 6: Feel thankful and full of gratitude. Express your gratitude to the universe.

Step 7: Do this twice a day and for 21 days to get better results , you can do it even for 66 days.

Mirror technique

Do you want to make the best out of your daily routine, yes, then you are at the right place? Each one of you use a mirror and you use it daily in your daily routine for getting ready. Now, it's time to use this very fond thing of yours to amplify the energy for your benefit.

In this technique no extra effort is needed, you just have to look yourself into the mirror, which should be a full-length mirror and set your intentions for yourself. Look at yourself, make eye contact with yourself and say your goals as you have already achieved and feel the happy vibrations in your body. So, in a way it's your self-admiration time, talk as much good you can about yourself and keep looking at yourself in the mirror. Since, you are totally head to toe in front of the mirror, what you think, say, feel, see and vibrate reflects back on you, and thus it amplifies whatever vibrations you give.

So, be very sure of your thoughts, what you think will reflect back on you and with a greater vibration, throw all good intentions here so that it amplifies and bounces back to you. Do this technique while doing your morning routine and night routine, while doing your skincare and target your subconscious mind for your greater benefits. It's really amazing, it will give you an instant boost of confidence every time you do so. All you need to do is go to a quiet, calm place with a mirror. Preferably it should be a full-length mirror, but if you don't have one, you can use any length so that you can see your face. Stand in a posture in which you feel empowered - put your shoulders back and lift your head with confidence. Centre yourself with a few deep breaths. Make an eye contact with yourself and start speaking,"I am...." , and say your affirmations, goals loudly to yourself. By doing this technique you will embody the vibrations you want to attract.

555 techniques

In this technique you have to think about your desires and dreams into affirmations you have written in the goal card and you have to allot a time for yourself to work on those affirmations every day, write your affirmations 55 times every day continuously for 5 days. You do this for 5 days and write 55 times, that's why it's called the 555 techniques. It's a very simple and effective technique to configure your subconscious mind. People have tried this technique and have accelerated the speed of their manifestations.

Thank you, technique, the gratitude attitude.

Don't miss even a single opportunity to thank the universe, be grateful to the universe as much as you can even for the smallest thing you possess and try to do this while in nature during your nature walks, be thankful and be full of gratitude.

What happens when you do this?

Remember the water technique, the positive vibrations were set and it formed a beautiful geometric pattern. The vibration of gratitude, praise, appreciation will make you vibrate at higher frequencies and hence you will attract positive vibrations toward yourself. Joy, happiness, blessings etc. Give gratitude and configure yourself for attracting all the good and positive things in your life. Your vibrations are like radio signals, if you emit AM frequency, you cannot tune in to the FM frequency. With gratitude your vibrations are in compatibility with that of the universe, and you attract like vibrations and you are aligned with the universe. Under the open sky and in nature you catch the vibrations more easily, so do it while walking in the garden to make better connection.

Remember, how you feel if someone says, "**Thank You**" to you, so spread this virus of thanking for everything in your life. **Gratitude should be your attitude.**

Visualization.

Visualisation is generally playing the reel of what you want in your life. Think and imagine the scene and it plays in your mind like a movie.

When you read the above-mentioned sentence, you get confused about what you are actually supposed to do, but it's really simple. Let's understand with an example.

Raju was a very poor boy; he worked hard and became an IAS officer. He has all the comforts in life now, but he very often slips into the memory of his childhood. In which he remembers, his father used to drop him to his school, in the days of flood, he used to sit on his father's shoulders and used to enjoy the ride. At a mere mention of thoughts like this, a reel plays in his mind and everything flashes like a movie.

This is exactly what visualization is, here I have mentioned about the past, the same thing, you have to do thinking about your future. You have to visualise yourself in the position you want to see yourself in future. Close your eyes, take two three deep breaths and jump into the future you want for yourself. It can be a sea facing bungalow, you riding a fancy car or holding a trophy of a pageant.

Yes, it can be anything you desire and dream. Try this miraculous exercise in the morning and at night before you sleep. It's an easy technique and changes life and fills you with all the positive thoughts and motivation.

369 techniques.

369 technique is used by many famous and successful people all around the world. This technique is very simple, all you have to do is to write or read your affirmations, but here you have to apply the 17 second rule to it, your affirmations should be as such that it takes 17 seconds, when you read it aloud or when you write it. You have to read this thrice in the morning, 6 times in the afternoon and 9 times before you sleep. This is a very powerful technique to retune your subconscious to achieve all that you have dreamt and desired.

All the techniques mentioned above are the techniques used to reprogram your mind and to configure it to receive all that you desire. Since, everything has vibrations, thoughts too have it, you just have to tune in to that frequency as you often do while tuning the radio.

When you perceive a thought and think about it continuously and repeat it again and again you start vibrating at that frequency and catch and set connections with all the things vibrating at that frequency and thus all manifestations come true.

Here is the story 'tune in the radio' that I have already published in my book "The Inklings" , read, enjoy and you can relate to it.

Tune in the radio

You tune in the radio to tune your favourite station. Driving without tuning in, the favourite FM has become a nightmare. When FM signals are lost the CD and the USB comes to our rescue. In this digital age, we have lots of options for listening to songs. Many apps are also available but when we turn on the radio, we tune in to the station we like. The station of our choice. We set the frequency to the radio station we want to listen to, as it soothes and matches our wavelength. The radio jockey adds charm to the radio station we like. We tune in to that station again and again.

Similarly, our universe is full of frequencies. Frequency of thoughts, good thoughts, bad thoughts, positive thoughts and negative thoughts

The type of thought our mind has, it coordinates with that frequency of the universe. If we think good, we pitch into the good frequencies, if we think bad, we match to the bad frequencies. This phenomenon of the universe is famously known as the law of attraction. What we think is what we attract. Before we start doing anything, it begins with a thought in our mind. First the thought clicks then the action is done.

Here is a beautiful story of thoughts of a common man Rohan.

Rohan, a fresher from an engineering college, who just got placed and has started living independently in the capital city of Delhi.

Rohan intended to buy the monthly groceries, he sat inside his car and tuned in to his favourite radio station. On the way to the grocery store which was in the mall, his eyes caught the attention of the dummy wearing a very smart t-shirt at a famous garment brand outlet. He just adored the amalgamation of the colour and the design of the t-shirt displayed. He had words of praise for that t-shirt in his mind. He appreciated the look and the design set on the display on the dummy. He couldn't hold on to his excitement and entered the store to check on the t-shirt. He checked the price and it seemed too expensive for him to buy at that moment. He just had a glance of that t-shirt on the dummy and captured the beautiful picture of it, in his mind and expressed his gratitude for the same. He sent his gratitude to the makers and the designers of the merchandising chain. He proceeded towards the supermarket to buy his groceries.

The impression of that t-shirt was deeply embedded in his mind and was not going off his mind. He bought the groceries, cross-checked the items purchased and left the mall to reach home.

He drove back happily and soon got busy in his office and household chores. One month passed, again a day came to get the groceries for the home. He made a list of items he needed to buy and proceeded to the same mall he visited last month. While going towards the supermarket, he crossed that brand outlet he checked last month. Suddenly, he noticed the store had a label of sale marked on it, he could not resist the offer and entered it to check the items on sale. His eyes were in search of that particular t-shirt which he liked so much last month. He checked all over and could not find it. He felt disheartened as he failed to spot it in the men's section. In a great disappointment, he advanced towards the exit of that store. Just before the exit, there was a box marked with "lucky sizes" in big bold letters.

The box itself denoted it was a box with left out single pieces of garment and that too at one-third of the price. Only the lucky ones who could fit into those sizes could buy them as there was no size choice available. Rohan checked the box and tried his luck. He saw the t-shirt in the box, pulled it out and checked the size. It was marked "s" on it. He jumped with joy, he got what he was looking for and that too in his size "small".

The moment was just magical. He took the T-shirt and advanced towards the billing section to make the payment. The t-shirt which was out of his budget just a few days back was available to him at one-third of its price. It seemed magical, but it was nothing but tuning of the frequency. His mind tuned in to the frequency of that particular garment and it was given to him by the universe.

Our mind is the receiving and the broadcasting station. Everything we desire is available in the universe, we just have to set the frequency to match it. Beware of your thoughts, if it's positive, it will shower positivity but if it's negative, it will engulf you in negativity and dump you in its filth. Keep tuning in the good stuff.

Magical pillow

Here is another story of magical pillow, read and explore the magic it does.

Sunday, a day full of fun for my family. On Sundays, we usually do all the chores together be it cleaning, washing clothes, pressing or refilling the groceries. Everything was almost done by the afternoon. Evenings are mostly spent with the family together and finally, at night we set the alarm to get up at 6 a.m. as Monday throws us all back to the set routine. It's only the weekend that we spend with the family together either doing the chores or enjoying the moment.

So, it's Sunday and my Mom and Dad are out of town and today I am at my Grandparent's house. The weekend was spent with love, care, and pampering from my Grandparents and now I am going to sleep, oh! I missed setting the alarm. I got up from the bed, my septuagenarian are sleeping, they must be wondering that am I in a search of an opportunity to do some mischief, but that is not the case, I am trying to find an alarm clock, it must be in the study room, it's dark and I am scared, so I quickly ran towards the study room, grabbed the alarm clock and ran back in full speed to the bedroom.

I am out of breath and was trying to grab some breath, my heavy breathing disturbed my Grandmother's sleep, she got up from her sleep a took a glance at me, I saw two big eyes like an owl glaring at me in suspicion, she asked, why so much activity is happening in the room at this hour, she inquired about the time from me, I turned the face of the clock towards me and it showed it was 5 a.m. I told her it's 5 and Grandma, smiled and said it can't happen. I checked the time and the clock showed the same time again. My Grandma smiled and said bring the clock, I ran towards her and she grabbed me into her arms. She gently made me sit on the bed and was looking at the clock by the window as some light was peeping into the room through the gaps of the curtain. She banged the clock twice and then said, the clock battery is dead and it is not working.

I was worried that if the watch is not working, how will I wake up tomorrow in the morning.

My Grandparents were Septuagenarian. So, I thought, I might miss getting up on time. My Grandmother pulled me towards her and grabbed me in her arms and said come let me teach you some magic. She was on her bed, she turned back, picked a pillow, and said this is a magical pillow, just give it a command to wake you up at whatever time you intend to wake up and it will wake you up at that exact time. I laughed at my Grandmother and said "Grandma, I know you want me to sleep, so you are trying this trick with me." She smiled and said just try it once and see the magic. I too believed that there is no harm in trying it. I held the pillow with both my hands and brought it close to my mouth and whispered ," hey, magical pillow, wake me up at 6 in the morning tomorrow.

A few minutes later I paced it on the bed and rested my head on it. I was thinking if it's magic, it's awesome, and with this thought, I slipped into a state of sleep. I woke up, it was morning and the birds were chirping. I was still in sleep mode. I left the bed and advanced towards my Grandfather's almirah. I took out his wristwatch to check the time, it was 6 a.m sharp.

I was amazed, the magic happened. I could not believe that it's real, so I thought, I would try it again tonight. With this thought, I started getting ready for school and left for school after some time.

In school, I got busy with my studies but whenever there was free time I thought about this magic, I was eager to share it with my friends but I controlled myself, I was not sure if it was really magic or if it happened by chance. I decided to try it for a week and only after getting assured about this,I intended to share it with my friends. I had a fear, if I share it and it fails, my friends will make fun of me, so I wanted to be doubly sure.

I came back from school and after finishing my lunch I did my homework, later in the evening I went out to play. I came from the field after playing a spectacular football match and saw my parents waiting in the living room.

I almost forgot that they will pick me today from my Grandparent's house. I spent some time with my aging Grandparents and went back home. Before leaving, I whispered into my Grandmother's ear," The magic happened Grandma". Though I told my grandmother it happened, but I was still not sure.

I was going to experiment it for seven days before I reached any conclusion.

So, every day at night, I would ask my pillow to wake me up at 6 a.m and I would also set an alarm for 6:10 as my backup. I was surprised all these 7 days, I woke up every day at 6 a.m sharp and would turn off the alarm.

It was really magic and I started believing it but one thought came to my mind that it's not magic, it's my habit of getting up at 6 a.m "This is not magic; this is my daily routine, I murmured." So, now I decided to change the set time and then experiment it again.

This time I had different time slots ranging from 5 a.m to 6 a.m. for Monday I kept it for 5 a.m, for Tuesday, I kept it for 5:30 a.m. For Wednesday it was 5:45 a.m. and so on.

To my surprise, the pillow passed the test, every day before sleeping I said " pillow wake me up at so and so time, and whatever time I announced, I woke up sharp at that time. The pillow has now passed the test. I very happily shared it with my friends. My friends tried this magical technique and were amazed at the result. I also told my parents about it. Both of them smiled at each other and told me it's nothing but the magic of the subconscious mind.

Try this magic technique for setting an alarm and also write your goal in a chit and keep it under your pillow every night before sleep and it will be an affirmation before sleeping.

Try this technique and show this magic to your children to amuse them.

"Training and managing your own mind is the most important skill you could ever own in terms of both happiness and success."-T. Harv. Eker

CHAPTER TWENTY

Be a verb, not a noun

You all are aware of what is a noun? The noun is basically the name of a person, place, or things around us. Now, let's quickly recapitulate what is a verb? Verbs are generally defined as the action words like jumping, eating, sleeping, etc. A verb actually defines the action done by the subject. In the book of life, you all are the nouns and the verb are your actions, so concentrate on the actions you do in your life and get known by your noun i.e., your name. In this great way, the noun and the verb are directly proportional to each other.

If you take the actions for your dreams, desires, and goals and give your heart and soul to it then nothing in this world can stop you from becoming successful i.e., from achieving what you want. The actions taken by you with persistence will surely bring to you the desired success.This reminds me of my childhood, I was very weak in mathematics and used to hate the subject, as I never scored good marks in it, and when I started taking action to improve, it happened magically.

Let's understand it with this example:

Actually, I failed in Maths as I scored below 40 percent and was sad and scared of getting scolded by my parents, there was fear in me. Fear of failure, fear of poor marks, fear of being judged, etc., etc. I very clearly remember, I reached home and after lunch, my father asked me about it and in a shaky voice, I announced my marks to him. I was scared, but what I was scared of (fear of being scolded by parents) never happened. Instead, my father understood and took me with him and showed me the earthen pot, kept on a big piece of stone in our kitchen. I thought he took me there to make me drink some water, as it was a scorching summer afternoon, but I was wrong.

His very purpose of taking me there was to show me the shape of the stone that has become concave, as the curve of the earthen pot was hitting it consistently for many years. Being a stone, a hard solid piece of rock, it got eroded and it took the shape of the base of the earthen pot that was a concave curve. This wasn't a miracle; this was the action taken daily by the earthen pot. It was daily filled with fresh water and was kept on that stone, the action of keeping it persistently there had resulted in the creation of that curve. With this example my father taught me about persistence and he explained to me that if you take actions daily to improve, you will improve, no matter how tough the task is.

"If an earthen pot that is weak and fragile that breaks down if it falls has a capacity to erode a tough and a hard stone, with its actions. Why can't you do the same? You all can also work on your weaknesses, no matter how tough the subject is." These were his words.

It was really an eye-opening lesson for me, I pledged to be responsible for my actions and started working on Mathematics, I practiced the sums daily and it became my habit very soon. In the next term exam, I scored full marks in Maths and was on cloud nine. My action made me famous in my class as the teacher too was glad to see my performance. My name was announced many times in the class as I had scored the full marks, my noun i.e. my name was known because of my actions.

It's rightly said, "Actions speak louder than words."

If you want to feel good, change your actions. If you feel less deserving check your actions as having any big desire without any actions is a complete sin. It is only your action that gives you either pain or pleasure. so, if there is pain in your life, check your actions and change them to change the way you want to feel.

Be the verb and not the noun. It's your actions that bring name and make you renowned and famous.

Focus on action and be persistent.

"Ambition is the path to success . Persistence is the vehicle you arrive in." - Bill Bradley.

CHAPTER TWENTY-ONE

Imagination

Imagination is something that does not need any preparation, just close your eyes and dip into the world of imagination. It will take nothing from you, doing this will only give you the wings to fly. Keep all your beliefs aside and go on your imaginative adventure to explore the world you want and see yourself in its possession. It will definitely fill you with joy, as well as fuel you with the energy to take the desired actions to accomplish, what you want.

Thomas Alva Edison has said that knowledge is less powerful than imagination or you can say imagination is more powerful than knowledge.

Now let's understand what knowledge is. ***Knowledge is basically a compilation of all the learnings that are around us based on our past experiences and experiments.*** The imagination on the other hand is completely imaginary things that are still not in existence around us. It's just available to us in the form of thought in our mind and acts as a seed. This seed of imagination grows and takes the shape of reality miraculously as our subconscious mind gets into the work of fetching the ways to make it true. Hence, these seeds of imagination are sowed in our mind, the ideas keep popping in and in some time the idea hits reality and the imagination turns into reality.

Let's understand that before airplanes were invented, the idea of flying as a bird in the sky must have brought so much disgrace to the thinkers of this idea. People must have termed them lunatics or mad just because they imagined this. This imagination was free from the past knowledge and hence had a power in it. The imagination came true after failing in many experiments conducted to make it a success. Now those people who had the tag of lunatic by the people around them are famous as the Wright Brothers.

Had there been no imagination, it would have been impossible to invent airplanes. In similar ways, many inventions are made by people who refused to work on the basis of knowledge and had great imaginative traits.

Napoleon Hill in his book, "Think and grow rich," has said that imagination is the workshop of the mind, where all dreams take shape and come to reality. Imagination is vital in the success of a person in any profession be it designing, science, acting, writing or anything else. Basically, all types of work done is based on just one key factor and that is our imagination.

The Vedas and the Upanishads along with other religious books like the Ramayana and Mahabharata were written by the sages and the saints who had great wisdom and their imagination were very rich. These books were written long back, many thousand years ago.

For e.g., if we talk about Ramayana the story of Lord Ram written by Valmiki Ji, he had mentioned in the Sita Haran episode (sita abduction episode) that Raavan, will come on the Pushpak viman (flying cart) from Lanka and would take Sita away. It was forecasted, Lord Ram would return to Ayodhya after his victory, in the Pushpak viman, it was a mere piece of imagination but this wisdom was not taken seriously by the Indians. On the other hand, the same imaginative powers were present in the Wright brothers who worked on it and airplanes were invented. If any Indian had taken this idea and he would have worked on it, then today our country would have been on the inventor's list.

Similarly, it was said by the great poet Ved Vyas ji 5000 years ago in Mahabharat that by sitting at a distance Sanjay will telecast the live commentary of the war of Kurukshetra to Dhritarashtra. It was all imagination but the same idea was tapped by some Russian scientist, and the invention of television took place. The list of examples does not stop here. Adding to the list, will be the work of Kalidas, another great gem of Indian soil. Kali das Ji in Meghdootam wrote around 2500 years ago that a man talks to the cloud and sends messages to his beloved wife, this imagination was also tapped and cloud computing and cloud storage were invented by Americans.

Imaginations have no relations with past knowledge as imaginations have no connection with the facts. Imagination is in fact free from any belief whether it is true or false. The potential of imagination should never be left untapped, if you ignore your imaginative power, and leave the idea that generated out of your mind, you are missing an opportunity to succeed in life. It's quite possible, someone else will use his or her imagination and would tap the same idea you had long back and will achieve success.

This happens many times if you notice, one idea comes to you and you fail to realize its potential. The same idea clicks to some other person and he taps it and uses it. He takes action and starts a start-up and later this start-up grows into a big business and eventually makes huge profits out of the same idea you had in the past and you failed to take action.

I hope none of you would now leave your imagination to rest, else it will rust. Instead, these examples will give more power and will instill more faith and courage to give wings to your imagination.

Albert Einstein once said,"imagination is more important than knowledge. Knowledge is limited, imagination encircles the world."

CHAPTER TWENTY-TWO

Get used to rejections

Since, you are on this journey of dream, desire, and destination, and now you have started taking actions so get used to rejections. For every successful attempt, one has to go through rejections. These rejections indicate two things: either the strategy is defective or the direction you are following is wrong. But while going through rejections you go through a self-refining process. The journey that is full of struggles gives you learning throughout your life. You adapt many ways to pave your path to success, and this hit-and-trial method gives you the wisdom on how to proceed towards your goals.

This very quality of finding new ways makes you unique from others and you discover a new path of doing the same things that others do, but in your unique way and that makes you, your own brand that surely differentiates you from the crowd. The haters and trollers get their answers with your success. This success does not come easy. Before all the trials of new methods, you have to fail a million times in private as well as in public before you reach the pinnacle of success.

A few examples of rejection followed by massive success are;

Walt Disney was rejected by a newspaper editor stating he lacked imagination.

Stephen King was rejected 30 times before he shot to fame in the writing world.

J K Rowling faced many rejections before becoming the bestselling Author.

William Golding yet another novelist failed many times but now listed amongst best novelists.

So be ready for rejections and get used to them. The world has stereotype thinking and that can be broken only with innovation and uniqueness that makes you stand out of the crowd.

Rejection is just like a rubber ball, the harder you hit the more it bounces back. If you hit the bottom phase of your life don't get disheartened because that is the lowest and the only option left is bouncing back in the opposite direction. After every low comes a high and after every failure there comes a success.

Focus on the destination and not from where you came, shred the past failures.

In the journey of dream desire and destination, your focus should be on the roadmap that paves the path to the point you want to reach. If you keep wandering in the old allies and don't take up the new route designed to reach a point you get stuck and lost there.

Let's take an example, sometimes while driving we take a wrong turn and keep on revolving in the same path again and again and when this realization comes that we are taking rounds at the same place then we seek help from people nearby and try to reach the destination. The same thing happens if we keep revisiting the old place again and again, we will never explore a new place. You have to take up a new route, a new path, and focus on it.

Everyone has a past and we can't deny this fact. Some people have a glorious past and keep revisiting it and there is no progress in their life later on because they seem lost and they are stagnant in life. Despite, being positive and talking positive things that had happened in the past, they seem fully satisfied with that time and situation and stop paving the way for success further.

On other hand some people have a difficult past, full of grief and sorrow they are badly stuck in their past, all they have are the memories of those hard times. Those hard times seem to be a roundabout of their life, it has 4 exits but they choose to revolve around it at that very point of the roundabout. These 4 exits give them the chance to change their path but these particular groups of people love going round and round at the same place. In such a case the starting and ending point is not defined and they start and end at the same point again and again and their life is wasted.

That is why, from where you have come becomes unimportant and focusing on where to go becomes very crucial. So, remember wherever life brings you at a roundabout don't take rounds there for a long time, rather focus on the exit and discover a new path that will be in any way better than being stuck there. Come out of this vicious circle of life where you get stuck at a point and keep taking rounds without realizing that a new path is available. This new discovery is only possible when you stop focusing on your past.

Stop complaining and cribbing. It's like a roundabout with no exit. You keep taking rounds there again and again and get stuck in the vicious circle of negativity.

Focus on the destination.

When you stop looking at your past, you will start focusing on the present moment, hence you will fetch ways to work on the new ideas that will give you more gateways to make yourself more positive and productive. This will gradually shift you in the positive frame of mind and will push you to focus on making progress. You will gradually hit a new area of abundance with your consistent actions and success will follow. You must focus on the action steps that you are planning to take to accomplish your goals rather than bragging of past success or crying over the past failure.

Give weightage to your dreams and not to memories.

Dreams are your future and memories are your past. The memories, if at all matter, should be the good ones in your mind. It must have the capacity to motivate you, rejuvenate you, and bring in the joys of your past. All bad and negative memories should be discarded and shredded from your storage system as they bring only suffering and resentment as you remember and go through the bad feeling again so it should be discarded permanently. Keep a room for only good memories so that you are filled with feelings of joy, of the time you are visiting in your memories and it gives you the power to grow more in the future.

Remember good things from the past but don't get stuck there as it will retard your progress in future dream projects. To achieve your dream, you need consistent hard work in the direction of achieving your dreams. To make your dreams come to reality, you have to show up every day to do a particular task, with the consistent hard work that comes only with discipline. You achieve your goals only with persistence and hence you hit your dream and it comes to reality, keep a focus on your dream and don't get lost in the achievements of your past. Those achievements are now a matter of the past and will motivate you for a small span of time but not be much fruitful in achieving your dreams.

It is just like walking five steps forward and walking four steps backward if you are stuck in memories. The progress gets retarded. So, keep an eye on your dreams and add five forward steps daily. These small steps seem small but help you come closer to your dreams every day by the steps you take each day in that direction, the direction towards achievements of your goals.

I am going to give one more example here is a little story to support it.

Radha, a call centre employee, had a night shift job. It was only the weekend she tried to make up for her sleep deficits so she hardly addressed the call bell at her home. Even if she heard she ignored it, but one day one of her friends dropped by to give her a surprise. She kept on knocking and pressing the call bell.

Radha was determined to ignore it but because the friend who dropped in to give her a surprise, kept on trying endlessly and one time Radha got so perturbed with the bell she came out of the bed and opened the door.

Here, two learnings are hidden in the story. First, be ready for rejection, and second, don't stop, be consistent in the effort. If you keep knocking on the door one day it will open. Here, knocking on the door is a persistent effort and opening the door is a success.

"The doors will be opened to those who are bold enough to knock."

-Tony Gaskins

CHAPTER TWENTY-THREE

Cancel the C's - clutter of your life

The C's are the clutter of your life and a great hurdle in the progress towards your goals. These are namely: Complaining, cribbing, criticism, and comparison. This clutter of your life occupies too much space in your life and makes you heavy.

I am sure each one of you must have seen the heavy vehicles on the national highways, these heavy vehicles only get permits to run on the highways post 10 PM and are not allowed to have transition during the day. These heavy vehicles cannot speed, if they do so they will lose their balance and will roll over, causing harm to themselves as well as to their surroundings. Similarly, if you have space for these c's in your life your progress will be retarded. If you try to speed in such a state, you will tremble down causing harm to yourself along with the people around you. It happens in real life too but to realize this, you need a very deep introspection and strong observations about yourself. So, it becomes vital to remove these c's from your life. The moment you shred these c's, more room will be created for good things in your life, like happiness and joy. The happiness and joy set you at the right vibrations and any act performed with love and joy makes the action easy. That's why, when one chooses the work that one loves as a profession, in such a case vocation is turned into vacation and you love your journey and reach your destination easily and effortlessly.

When the habit of criticizing and complaining is shredded from your mind then your intention is set in the right direction i.e. on your goals and as time passes, you focus more and more on your goals and the c's that were a part of your life disappears and is replaced by powerful habits needed for accelerating your speed towards your set target. Isn't it wonderful? Your energy that was draining in the handling of these c's are now preserved and directed towards your ultimate goal.

It is said energy flows where attention goes. Now this shift, where you have shredded the c's of life and you adapted to focus only on the goals, you are channelising your energies in the correct direction. This energy was also previously available but was wasted in the handling of the c's of life.

Now, as the new channel through which this energy flows with new positive intentions, it starts to show up results that seem to be a miracle to you. It's not at all a miracle but it is just putting in the scattered energies to a particular point to give a positive result as the intentions set were positive.

To understand the focus in a better way, there is a story.

This story supports the theory, "energy flows where attention goes."

There was a man who was troubled because people talked bad about him. Instead of ignoring such gossip, he channelized his energy in finding, why people talked bad about him? He wasted a huge amount of time in finding it. As a result, his productivity declined and his peace of mind was also taken away. One day he told this to his employer and handed over his resignation to him, citing this silly reason. The employer laughed at such a small problem and asked the employee (who was all set to resign) to hold a glass of water in his hands and while holding it, he asked him to take a tour of the full office so that he can have this tour in his memory after resigning and he could also find who were those people, who talked bad about him.

The glass was full, till the top and the employer added that he will accept his resignation only on one condition, not a single drop should spill from the glass while moving around in the office.

The employee thought it was such an easy task, he started but soon realized it needed his full focus, so maintaining his full focus on the glass, he took a tour and very carefully completed it and reached the employer's cabin. The employer congratulated him and inquired, who were those people who talked bad about him. The employee answered, his focus was on the glass, so he could not find who those people were and what they were talking about. The employee was completely unaware and had no idea of the gossip going on about him. What they talked about and who were such people hardly caught his attention, as he focused on the glass of water.

The employer smiled and said, " See, your focus was on the glass of water and you prevented water from spilling." As your focus was on it, you could not hear, what other people were gossiping about you. The energy flows where you focus and this is the right attitude to live life.

Keep your focus free from the c's of life, as they are the biggest roadblocks in your journey towards achieving your dreams and in reaching the destination.

It happens many times what others say and thinks catches your attention, don't focus on it rather focus on your goals.

In this journey, when you deviate or break the rules the challans should also be imposed, in the same way, as while driving any vehicle, you get it issued on breaking the traffic rules. The only difference is, here you have to be your own guard, whenever you criticize, compare or crib about anything in life, whenever you are on the wrong side, while you are on the way to success, this challan must be imposed to drive you again on the positive path and shred the negativity. Put a check on yourself whenever you give entry to these c's in your life. Every time you use these c's pay fine for it, and use that fund in some social cause, very soon you will get rid of these c's with a good feeling because as you attach a purpose of contributing that penalty(fine) fund for a social cause, it will give you more energy to shred the c's very fast.

Free yourself from the baggage of the complaints, comparisons, cribbing and discover new freedom of your life and pick up speed to hit your destination.

Champions never complain, they are too busy getting better - John Wooden

Complaining only takes away and never solves the problems for tomorrow- James Alttucher

When you complain you make yourself a victim, leave the situation or accept it, all else is madness - Echart Tolle

CHAPTER TWENTY-FOUR

Power of decision

Power of Decision

You have the power to change your life only if you have the power of decision-making. Decision-making is very crucial; it makes rags to riches and vice-versa. The power of taking decisions can lift you to heights and if the decision goes wrong, it throws you on the ground.

You set goals and start thinking of achieving them but procrastinate in doing so by the postponement of the task. Why this happens? The only probable reason for doing so is the lack of action. But before action, comes the power of decision. If you have not decided firmly on your goals then, you lack the action steps. It can be said that action is very closely knitted with your decision. It gives you the power to take action towards your goal.

Taking prompt decisions gives you the ability to reach your goal in time, if you delay in taking a decision your journey towards your goals, gets retarded. Promptness in decision making is a strength as you can grab many opportunities with this trait, but once you take decision be slow in changing it and stick to it. If you fail to stick to a paticular decision, you keep hopping and changing decisions and thus fail to set a strong goal. You will get the results only if you stick to your decisions.

The next question arises, why people lack the ability of decision-making?

Decision-making is almost missing in around 90% of the people, and this is the sad truth. Let's go deep to find this. The main reason behind the lack of the power of decision-making is mostly related to fear of criticism, and fear of being judged. We all think deeply about what others will think. Apart from this, there is deep conditioning of our mind for a very long time. Since childhood, the decision is always taken by our elders, mostly father or mother. Gradually as you grow this thought sets a neuron pattern and builds your self-image. It develops a firm self-image and a belief and we all fear to break that set pattern. Yes, the power of decision-making is directly related to self-image. So, if you want to develop the power of decision making, you must build a strong self-image.

When you lack the power of decision making, you drift from one path to the other as you are driven by the influence of other people around you. These people are none other than your friends and family. Since, the power of decision rests on others, you indirectly hand over the steering wheel of your life to them, and this causes major havoc in your life.

Remember, in this journey of your dreams, desire to your destination the most important part is you, as I mentioned in chapter 2. You are on the journey to reach your goals, and your body and mind are the vehicles in which you are traveling. How can you hand over the steering wheel of your vehicle to any other person? Think about this wisely.

Our life is not a video game. In the game generally, you have three lives or maybe more. So, if there is a mistake, you have a chance to accommodate that mistake too. If you are playing too well, you earn points and even earn back the lost life but sadly in real life, there is no such arrangement. That is why decision-making becomes so important and crucial.

You have to take charge of your life and it should be planned well. One cannot plan everything hundred percent but can make a conscious effort to do so, and this comes with the power of decision-making. Whatever happens in your life, only you are responsible for it. It will be unwise to hold someone else responsible for all the wrongs in your life. And if it is so, you are not a tree and you are free to move to a place of your choice finding solace. In order to do so, it again needs the power of decision making.

When we go out on the road and see the vehicles, each vehicle has its own independent driver. The driver drives the vehicle according to his or her own wisdom and consciousness and no driver handles or drives someone else's vehicle. In case of a breakdown of the vehicle, the vehicle is towed or is supported by other vehicle's driver for the correction of the errors in the machine for making it fit for driving. After the rectification of the errors in the machine, it's handed over to the driver for further use. If no support is found, the vehicle is either taken for correction by the driver himself to the garage, anyhow with lots of difficulties. Either the vehicle reaches garage or in case of the incapability of the driver to do so, it is dumped there itself. In due course of time, the vehicle rusts and is just a piece of junk for everyone.

Your life is just like that, you have to be the driver of your own life. If something goes wrong your family and friends can just support or give advice for the rectification of the errors, but the power of decision rests with you. After all, you have to lead your own life independently based on your own decisions, according to your wisdom.

So, hold the steering of your life and drive swiftly.

The starting point of your life is the birth and the destination is the death what lies in between is the drive, how one drives all the way throughout the journey matters, here the starting point is your dreams and the destination is your goal. When the road is good ie situations are favourable you can glide the vehicle on full speed and accelerate with good habits as they are the catalyst but you must be cautious, when the roads are rough ie when you have bad habits, you procrastinate, compare, and criticize. Hold the steering of your vehicle and drive safely. Glide when the road is smooth and be cautious when its rough and do remember to fasten your seat belts.

Determination - the will power.

The will power is the powerhouse of your mind. Any act before it is performed is first conceived in your mind. The will power and the consistency together build the determination. There is nothing called luck. One makes his own luck through the hard work that comes totally from determination.

When a person ties himself to a goal and has full focus, with full determination , the unachievable becomes achievable.

A person who is determined has no room for self-pitying. The aim is of utmost importance for such a person. The determination to achieve the set goal is the central goal of such a person. The scope of worries, troubles, fears, doubts diminishes and the room for positive attributes magnifies and provides strength to the individual to achieve the set goal.

The strength grows day-by-day and it can be developed only by putting effort and practice. Determination just acts as a workout that strengthens the muscles you train. The more determined you are, towards the goal the more power you get to achieve the same. Determination needs the heart, body and soul together into the purpose to be achieved. If one puts in the heart, body and the soul, the chances of failure of that purpose becomes very bleak. Determination is the fuel on which the desire runs successfully to reach its destination. Determination is the aspiration, it comes only after perspiration.

You perspire and get what you aspire for.

Destination

Destination is the goal post where the target is hit to achieve it. In case of an unstable and indecisive mind the goal post is not in a picture throughout life. A person starts the journey without knowing where to go. Such a person has got no navigation in his life. Such a person travels hay-way in confusion here and there without any idea, where to reach. This type of mindset is prone to more struggles. The planning is missing. Along with the struggles the pain of life magnifies manifolds and many uninvited and unanticipated things pops-up to add to the pain to convert it into a poison. The lack of planning results in the poor handling of one's life. The purpose of life is lost and the bare need remains stuck just to the basic needs of food, shelter and clothing.

The basic need of food, shelter and clothing is for all the individuals but the quality of it defines the journey one goes through. Life is a race and birth and death are the starting and the ending points. You all start this race at the time of birth and also reach the end when you die. How you run, right from the start matters. When you start good, putting all the energy, and get exhausted in the middle and give up, you never reach the destination. Maintaining a rhythm (consistent efforts) throughout is necessary to reach the destination. Now to reach the destination the desire and determination must go hand in hand to strike the goal of life i.e. the destination.

Decision making is linked with determination as only after a firm decision, determination to work in the form of action starts, and once determination keeps rolling you reach your destination.

Decision is the ultimate power. Decisions shape destiny -Tony Robbins

CHAPTER TWENTY-FIVE

Conclusion

The journey of dream, desire, and destination has many vital components. Basically, the most important thing is goal-setting with a definite timeline as a goal without a timeline, it is just a wish. The goal-setting gives you a clear picture of the point, till which you want to travel. The travelling point is decided only if you weigh our dreams and desires minutely and after that, you decide to take steps to reach that point henceforth decision of a person comes into play. The decision taken must be firm and only a firmness in the decision will give you the courage to take steps as actions to walk on that decided path on which you want to walk. Walking towards your decided goal will need repeated actions every day to reach the point you are intending to reach, it's not easy. It will take lots of courage and discipline to walk on this path with full faith that you are aiming to accomplish (your set goal). With these repetitions a discipline is set that can be followed only through the planning of a to-do list daily (to-do list will set discipline) and the willpower muscle will be strengthened. On this path, many hurdles will come and with courage, discipline, and persistence you will knock off the hurdles easily to reach your destination.

All this will need a very strong mindset as a strong mind is a well-trained mind. In a nutshell all you need are dreams, plans, goal setting, persistence, good habits, hardwork put together minus the c's of your life. **For all this, you have to strongly believe in your abilities and you have to take actions.**

As Dale Carnegie said in his book "Stop worrying start living" that "virtually everything we do is to change the way we feel, but we don't know how to do this."

The answer to this question is defined in Tony Robbins's book, "Awaken the giant within you" in which he says, "If you want to change your feelings, you must change your actions."

I was watching a video of some event in which our former president, Late Abdul kalam Ji was the chief guest and a school girl asked him the mantra of success. The mantra shared by him had four key components, these were:

1. **To have an aim.**
2. **To have a zeal to continue acquiring knowledge.**
3. **To be ready for the hard work.**
4. **To adapt perseverance.**

Anyone who has these 4 traits can strike success easily and reach the desired destination i.e. the goal.

So, if you are worried about your future and have a bad feeling associated with your past failures, don't get disheartened just follow the 4 mentioned key steps, and soon you will change your feelings.

Robert Kiyosaki has said, "The single most powerful asset we have is our mind, if it is trained well, it can create enormous wealth in what seems to be an instant."

So, train your brain to see good, act positively and consistently and yield positive outcomes.

This Sanskrit shloka from Brihadaranyaka Upanishad rightly describes the journey of dreams, desires, and destination beautifully.

"Kaama maya evayam purusha iti Sa Yatha kaamo bhavati tat kratur bhavati
Yat kratur bhavati tat karma kurute, Yat karma kurte tad abhisam padyate"

It means:

"You are what your deep driving desire is, as your desire is so is your will, as your will is so is your deed, as your deed is so is your destiny."

I sincerely hope that in this journey, I have made you aware of all the paths, that you have to go through, to reach your destination and you will reach your destination with an ease.

Success is the sum of small efforts-repeated day in and day out.-Robert Collier

Dreams are the seedlings of your future, nurture it and see it flourishing into reality.

Goal List

A goal without a timeline, is just a wish.

List your top 10 goals.

Project "me"

You are the most important project of your life. List the activities you do, to improve yourself.

To Do List

List all activities you intend to do with a time slot. Make a List, on the basis of importance and urgency of the task. Remember if you fail to plan you are planning to fail.

List your good and bad habits and the ways to use good habits to speed up your journey and ways to get rid of bad ones.

Snooze Button

List all moments when you procrastinate, set rewards to cancel it.

"Procrastination is the enemy of success."

Progress Report

If there is no struggle there is no progress. Step out from your comfort zone.

Measure your progress because , what can be measured can be improved.

Victory

"A journey of a thousand miles begins with a single step."

List your 100 wins big or small. Small wins everyday combines to become massive one day.

Gratitude

Adapt the attitude of gratitude. Thank for everthing you have in your life.

Say thank you for all big and small things in your life. Remember how it feels, when someone says, Thank You" to you. Make it viral and contagious.

Printed by Libri Plureos GmbH in Hamburg,
Germany

9 798885 465434